THE
SPORTING
CRAFTSMEN

THE
SPORTING
CRAFTSMEN

A complete guide to

contemporary makers

of custom-built

sporting equipment

ART CARTER

Countrysport Press
New Albany, Ohio

This edition of *The Sporting Craftsmen* was printed by Walsworth Publishing Company, Marceline, Missouri. The book was designed by Angela Saxon of Saxon Design, Traverse City, Michigan. It is set in Galliard, a typeface modeled on the work of Robert Granjon, a sixteenth-century letter cutter whose typefaces are renowned for their beauty and legibility. The special limited edition of this book is bound in Cabra leather and available in a signed and numbered edition of 250 copies.

Parts of this book have appeared in somewhat different form in *Sporting Classics* magazine. Reprinted with permission.

Published by Countrysport, Inc., 15 South High Street, P.O. Box 166, New Albany, Ohio 43054-0166

Printed in the United States of America

ISBN 0-924357-46-0 Trade Edition
ISBN 0-924357-47-9 Deluxe Limited Edition of 250

CONTENTS

ACKNOWLEDGEMENTS

Heartfelt thanks to the people whose help has been a tremendous resource and inspiration:

To my family, Maureen, Jessica, and Kevin, who have put up with the numerous boxes of stuff cluttering our house and my days away doing journalistic things when I might have been at home.

George Herron, knifemaker, who for the past twenty years has taught me what true craftsmanship is and that even if an individual is well-known or indeed, even famous, it is possible for him to be honest, sincere, generous, and a genuinely nice person.

Shelly Spindel, trusted and dear friend, who knows more about sporting collectibles than any other ten people I know and has always been willing to share his knowledge.

Doug Truax, editor of this book, who has been patient and professional throughout the metamorphosis of the work, which, it seemed, like bubble gum, got bigger the more we chewed on it.

And, to all of the craftsmen who refused to let "good enough" be in their vocabulary.

PREFACE

I love all of the "stuff" that is connected to hunting and fishing. I use it, collect it, and get a great deal of pleasure out of owning it. Some of these items are among my most prized possessions. If they are handmade by some craftsman, be he a renaissance man with the vocabulary of a thesaurus or some crusty curmudgeon loath to accept anyone in his cluttered workshop, then these objects are all the more more intrinsically valuable. And they become increasingly collectible with each passing year, which in these days of mass-produced and sometimes poor quality equipment, is truly worthy of admiration.

It is both a passion and a sense of respect that draws us to the beautifully handcrafted treasures that represent our finest hunting and fishing equipment and to the artisans who make them.

There are a number of common threads that connect such desirable implements as bamboo fly rods, fly reels, custom classic and precision hunting rifles, fishing flies, re-creations of historic muzzleloading rifles and fowlers, waterfowl calls, custom knives, and traditional longbows and recurves.

The first is that they are functional art. Perhaps in no other period in history have more skilled craftsmen produced such wonderful tools for our sport. Many of their creations are the best in their field; they should not only be used in rivers and coverts but, I believe, displayed in museums of art. Yet, in most cases, they are designed to be used. It is the very reason for their creation.

Therein lies another common ground, the quest for the better mousetrap. To the consummate craftsman his product must perform better than any other while reflecting his artistic interpretation. It is a matter of pride.

I have always been drawn to folks who are good with their hands. My father was such a man. He worked an honest hard day's work every day of his life, something I increasingly admire as I get older. Hands are something that I always notice about a craftsman. Usually they are rough and cracked from difficult work, invariably large and strong yet capable of lovingly producing the most demanding workmanship. The owners of these hands have an appreciation for beauty but they do not shy away from what it takes to build a superior product. Great craftsmen possess an indomitable spirit to do their best every time. They have a sense of history and heritage and a true love of their sport.

When you take possession of their work, they feel it should not only give you pleasure and faithful service, but should also serve your children and grandchildren well. Their endeavors are to be appreciated more than ever. Today, those of us who love to hunt and fish probably have less time to enjoy our pastimes than ever before. Therefore, handmade sporting equipment is not meant just for meat gathering, although it is often superlative for that task, but also to be admired as we use an extraordinary piece of equipment.

The purpose of this book is to introduce to you many of the splendid craftsmen I have come to know and respect over the years. They have taught me a great deal. Or contact the organizations shown under the Sources section at the back of the book; they will be happy to direct you to other fine craftsmen working in their fields. Look some of them up and examine their work. You will be glad you did.

Columbia, South Carolina
July, 1994

BAMBOO
FLY RODS

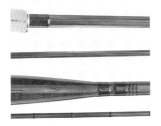

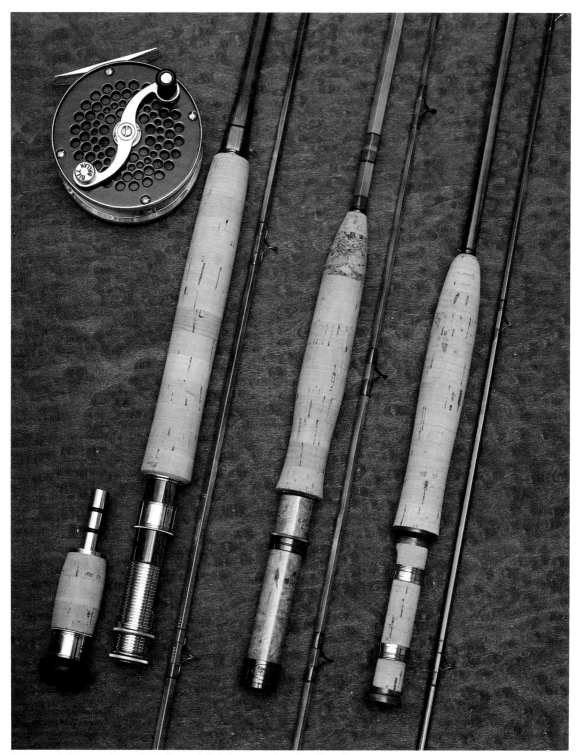

Thomas & Thomas, Kane Klassics, and Bob Summers bamboo fly rods.

BAMBOO
FLY RODS

On the other side of the world a miracle of nature grows tall and straight. Its strength and resiliency are born of howling monsoon winds that sweep off the Gulf of Tonkin and the South China Sea. Like an army of stoic emerald-green sentinels, stalks of forty-foot-high bamboo bend in the wind, ever resistant, always springing back to their original stance.

This singular bamboo, one of one thousand species which grow around the globe, is treasured above all others by those who fashion it into fine split-cane fly rods. Its common name is Tonkin cane, although it is called tea stick bamboo by the farmers who harvest it in Kwangsi Province. More properly its Latin name is *Arundinaria amabilis*, which loosely translated means "the lovely reed."

Bamboo has been utilized for centuries for everything from food and medicine to suspension bridges, kitchen utensils, and even by Thomas Edison in 1880 as a carbonized filament for his first light bulb. But its ultimate form occurs when a craftsman splits the Tonkin stalk, or culm, into six triangular strips, tapers them to tolerances within .001 inch, then glues them together into a solid hexagonal stick which tapers from a butt about the size of your little finger to a tip no larger than a pencil lead. For nearly 150 years this method has produced some of the most exquisite fishing tools ever devised.

In the early part of the nineteenth century fishing rods were made of woods like greenheart, lancewood, snakewood, purpleheart, ash, and others. Samuel Philippe, a gunsmith from Easton, Pennsylvania, is credited by most historians for making and selling the first split-cane rods in 1846. Hiram L. Leonard of Bangor, Maine, called the father of the modern cane rod, was using six-strip construction by 1874. After them came master craftsmen like Payne, Edwards, Thomas, Gillum, Halstead, Powell, Orvis, Dickerson, Garrison, Young, and many others.

Today fine bamboo fly rods incorporate impeccable work-manship and top-quality components. They are finished with the finest tung oil varnish or impregnated with resins to make them impervious to moisture. Some rods are hand planed on tapered forms made of hardwood or steel; for others, the strips are milled to fine tolerances on precision machines. The bamboo is heat tempered in an oven or over open flame for extra strength and resiliency, changing the molecular structure of the natural resins.

This tempering alters the color of the cane, depending on temperature and length of time. A few rods, like vintage Leonards and Winstons, turned a lovely golden tan or the color of ripe wheat. A number of other historical rods, like those crafted by Payne, reached a rich glowing brown. Orvis rods were darker still, like burnished mahogany. Paul Young rods had a distinctive mottled finish from his unique flame tempering. Modern day rodmakers achieve the same range of glowing colors.

Most fine rodmakers today wrap the guides with ultrafine silk thread in delicate hues of claret, olive, butter yellow, or brilliant Chinese red as well as the warm tans and browns displayed in the feathers of a ruffed grouse.

Rod actions vary from the slow wet-fly designs created by the early makers to fast-tipped sticks for dry flies to full- or semiparabolics for those who prefer a more relaxed casting motion and a rod that flexes all the way into the grip. Lengths range from tiny midge rods of less than 6 feet to powerful 9- or 10-foot casting tools for Atlantic salmon.

Cane rods made by master rodmakers of the golden age (1930 through the early 1960s) are prized by fishermen and avid collectors who pay many thousands of dollars for rare pieces. Today we are enjoying a reawakening in the craft of bamboo rodmaking, and perhaps the beginnings of a new golden age. Modern craftsmen are producing rods that are every bit the equal of those from years gone by; a few are the finest ever made.

Of all the individuals crafting fine rods today or in any other time period, Marc Aroner of Conway, Massachusetts, is at the head of the list. His workmanship and finish are undoubtedly the most admired when I discuss bamboo with other makers and dealers. His exquisite, fine-tipped rods approach the pinnacle in light, dry-fly design.

Aroner has been a full-time professional rodmaker since 1973, when he began working at Thomas & Thomas under Tom Dorsey and Tom Maxwell, two of the most respected makers of the modern era. Six years later he joined the famous H.L. Leonard Rod Company in Central Valley, New York, where he again worked with Tom Maxwell. Two years later he began producing rods under his own name.

Aroner's rods reflect a Leonard influence. He cuts his tapers on the old Leonard beveler which he now owns. His Hunt Pattern Series features rods which have a beautiful dark flame-tempered color. Nodes (growth rings in the bamboo) are hand-filled and pressed, and tips are book-matched so they will be identical. Finish, as on all his rods, is a flawless glassy spar varnish. Models range from a three-piece 6-foot rod for 3-weight line to an 8-foot for 6-weight line. The tip of the 6-footer is an incredible .046 of an inch thick (that's six pieces of tapered bamboo glued together into a perfect hexagon!).

His Spring Creek Series is a blonde version of the Hunt pattern and is wrapped in a green-olive silk, with a mortised reel seat of figured maple. If there is a more beautiful rod, I have yet to see it.

Aroner also makes a slightly lower-priced Fishing Creek Series that offers a medium action. He also has a line of special-order rods and even makes a couple of models with full intermediate wraps.

Considering the quality of his work, Aroner prices his rods very reasonably — currently from just over $1,000 to $1,295 for normal models. Special-order rods range up to $2,500. Best of all, if you were to order an Aroner rod today, you could possibly get delivery before next fishing season. That's not bad for rods that will one day become classics.

For a quarter of a century the words Thomas & Thomas have been synonymous with the finest bamboo rods. A tradition of excellence was born in 1969 when T&T opened its doors and began taking orders for a line of split-cane fly rods that have become the standard by which all others are judged.

Thomas & Thomas is named for Thomas Dorsey, a former doctoral student in philosophy at the University of Maryland, and Thomas Maxwell, a student at Kent State, who decided that it was time to make elegant cane rods every bit the equal of those built by the master rodmakers of the past.

They crafted their first professional rods in Chambersburg, Pennsylvania, but in 1972 moved to Greenfield, Massachusetts, where they purchased equipment and an extensive stock of aged

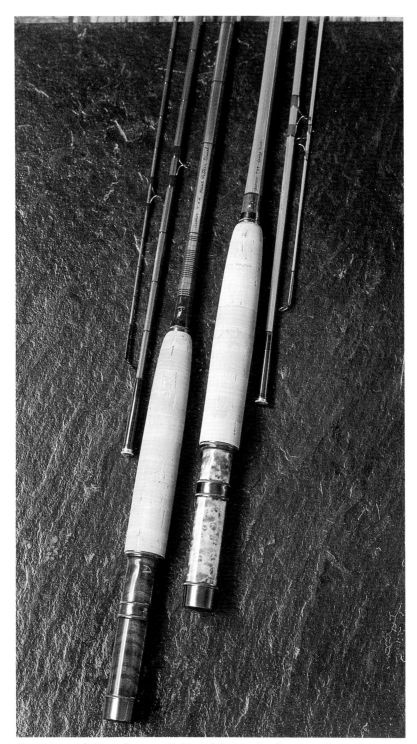

Marc Aroner's Hunt Pattern (left) and Spring Creek series rods.

Tom Dorsey checking the fine tolerances of a bamboo strip.

pre-embargo bamboo culms (purchased before the Cold War embargo with China after WWII) from retiring rodmaker Sewell N. Dunton. They went to work and in 1974 moved the business to nearby Turners Falls. Recently T&T moved into new and spacious quarters overlooking the Connecticut River, a few blocks down the street from their old shop.

Sixteen years ago Maxwell left the business and took over the famous H.L. Leonard Rod Company in New York. Dorsey has been the master rodmaker at the T&T shop since and has designed many exquisite rods. Once again there are two Toms at T&T. Tom Moran, a master craftsman from England whose rods have been sold all over the globe, has now joined the firm as a rodmaker and designer.

The T&T line is extensive. Top-of-the-line cane models are the Individualists. Made of complex tapers, they require forty-five hours of handwork to fashion the immaculate cane, burled walnut, and nickel silver into superb fishing tools. These exquisite rods have been given as presentation gifts for heads of state and royalty. In 1981 President Reagan commissioned an Individualist as a gift to Australia's Prime Minister Malcom Frazer and in 1982 a brace of rods for the Prince and Princess of Wales. Over the years such luminaries as actors Jack Lemmon, Robert Mitchum, and William Conrad, comedian George Carlin, rock star Eric Clapton, and the late big-band leader Benny Goodman have ordered rods from the New England rodmaker.

Individualists feature the distinctive T&T swelled butt and an impeccable high-gloss varnish finish. They are available in many sizes and tapers, from a tiny 6-footer for 4-weight to an $8\frac{1}{2}$-foot salmon rod for 8-weight.

The Classic line of Thomas & Thomas cane rods boasts a medium dry-fly action and a hand-buffed phenolic resin finish that is impregnated into the cane. Two-tip Individualists currently cost $1,650 and one-tip Classics are $985. My first honest-to-goodness fine bamboo rod was a wonderful 7-foot Classic made out of the pre-embargo cane during the early

Tom Moran flame-tempering bamboo culm.

Moran splitting the culm.

Tom Dorsey binding six strips of cane into a hexagonal rod.

T&T era. I wish I still had it, but I foolishly let some fast-talking horse trader beat me out of it. There is also a super lineup of graphite rods that cover the waterfront from little trout models for small streams to powerful sticks for the biggest saltwater denizens.

In 1979 Tom Dorsey began crafting a yearly Limited Edition Series, with his first effort celebrating the company's tenth anniversary. Each year since he has designed a unique creation in the rodmaker's art, sometimes as a one-of-a-kind rod and other years as a small limited edition. These rods have to rank among the most important and superb examples of bamboo rodmaking in history. All have become instant collector's items and have increased in value. In 1994, to celebrate the firm's twenty-fifty anniversary, he and Moran are making fifty rods with tiger-striped flamed cane to match a curly maple/cork reel seat.

Tom Dorsey, though still a young man of fifty-four, has already taken his place as one of the finest artists to have ever worked in the demanding creative medium called bamboo. He feels, as most creative people do, that it takes a certain kind of ego to be successful. "There is an innocence in the kind of ego found in people who create things. They are taking nothing from anyone," he says reflectively. "It is okay to be proud in that sense, to actually do something ideal—the Olympic skater, the baseball pitcher who goes to the Hall of Fame, and the rodmaker who makes a beautiful rod, the painter, architect, musician—to pursue excellence."

It has been a rewarding life for him, a man who gravitated to cane rodbuilding through an earlier love of classical endeavors. "I feel I am a wealthy man. I feel privileged to be able to do what I do, as a rodmaker and my life in fishing," he says respectfully. "I feel really fortunate because I have been able to be a jazz musician and to pursue the study of philosophy. I have loved all those things and have done them with a vengeance. If I am going to do it, I'm all the way!"

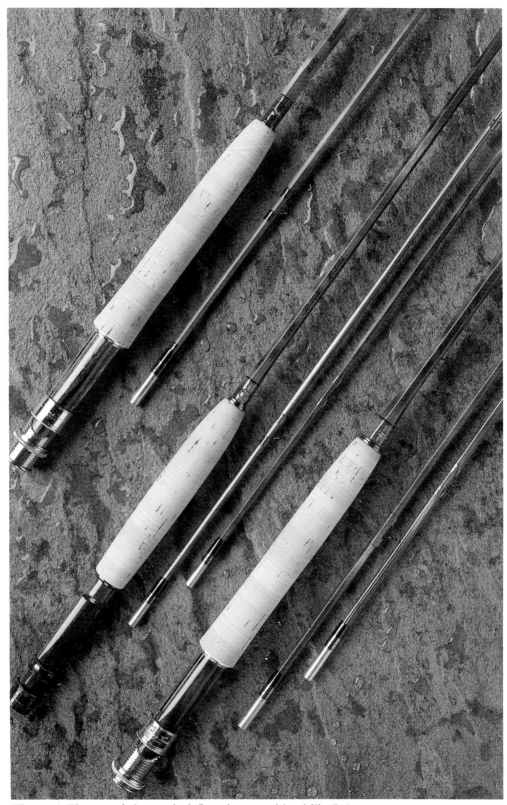

Thomas & Thomas rods feature dark flamed cane and jewel-like fittings.

As a young man Dorsey, who played bass with several jazz groups, found old musical instruments and restored them because money was tight in the early years of his musical career. Cane rods were the same for him. They were beautiful and eminently desirable but financially unattainable. Unless he made them. "I used to pick up old basses and restore them before I made rods. I've always been inclined to work with my hands. My father was a carpenter. I grew up doing things with my hands. It was always something about the smell of varnish and the wood. There is a common denominator in both. It emanates from wooden instruments, and from bamboo rods. I knew I wanted to have one but I was a student then. I guess it was a natural thing. If you enjoy fine things then you grow to appreciate bamboo rods. The thing to do was to make them so that I could have one."

The work of one of the greatest rodmakers was Dorsey's benchmark. "When I saw a rod by Jim Payne it was an inspiration to me. Because Payne was not simply a rodmaker, but his execution was impeccable. Not from the point of view of tapers necessarily, but the craftsmanship. They were truly beautiful."

Rod design has always been Dorsey's thing. It is one of the reasons, along with gorgeous finish work, that T&Ts are so highly thought of.

"I'm a design freak. I love messing around with tapers," Dorsey admits. "Bamboo is a heavy material and it keeps rodmakers honest. It has the disadvantage of weight (when compared to graphite or fiberglass) so tapering is everything. A few thousandths here and there can make an enormous difference. I think the greatest challenge for me in bamboo was to make rods that allow for a perfect presentation."

Tom Moran is now the second rodmaker at T&T. When he worked in Britain he had the reputation among knowledgeable aficionados as the best cane builder in Europe and indeed one of the best in the world. Most of his production in England

Putting the final varnish coat on rod wraps.

went to Japan and the United States. When Dorsey met him on a trip to Great Britain he knew Moran was a perfect fit for the Turners Falls company. "I had heard a lot about him," Dorsey says. "He is quite a rodbuilder. He was more of an American rodmaker with the varnish, finish, and aesthetics of his rods. Really beautiful stuff. I knew he would be part of the family immediately. He wanted to come here. He knows fly fishing and fly rods. He is quite a spokesman for bamboo. Not only is he a rodmaker, he is a polished mind in tune with the aesthetics of good things."

High praise indeed. And Moran gives Dorsey much of the credit for his maturation as a rodmaker of quality. "I had been making rods and then I became aware of American rods. Then when I saw a T&T it made me sick. I realized that at the time I wasn't even in kindergarten. I saw that Dorsey had brought to it a new grace when it looked as if bamboo had no future. His philosophy showed in his work and it just knocked my socks off."

The British maker also gives credit to another famous rodmaker who looked at his work early on and told him that though his cane work was above reproach he needed to understand more about what tapers could do for a good rod.

"That was a damn good lesson," Moran laughs. The advice he took to heart, like his favorite Shakespeare quotation: "What sweeter the uses of adversity. For like the toad, ugly and venomous, yet wears a precious jewel in its head." He is now the consummate student of what makes a good rod.

Moran is also sold on bamboo. "It's the classic material," he says, fingering an unfinished stick that he is in the process of straightening. "This wonderful material is the stiffest-to-weight material on Earth. If it were not for *Arundinaria amabilis*, if it were some species of spruce or larch or something, then that would be the classic rod. Bamboo is the constant. Everything else is on the guy who makes it."

Dorsey also feels that cane rods epitomize the best in the sport. "Bamboo is an icon of fly fishing—a link with the past."

As T&T celebrates its silver anniversary as a premier bamboo rodbuilding company, it is obvious that its cane rod production is in the hands of two masters.

Walt Carpenter of Huntington Mills, Pennsylvania, is one of the last active rodmakers to have come from the Hudson Valley-Catskill school of rodmaking. From just after the Civil War until today names synonymous with fine rods have come from this area—names like Leonard, Hawes, Thomas, Edwards, and Payne. The name Carpenter must be added to the list of great rodmakers.

A native of the Keystone State, Carpenter has been building beautiful classic rods for more than a quarter of a century.

He worked at the famous benches of the H.L. Leonard Rod Co. in New York for five years and then was rodmaker and manager of the E.F. Payne Rod Co. until it closed. Carpenter remained in New York from 1980 to 1989 building rods under his own name.

In his early years there he made a valuable friendship which helped launch his career as a rodmaker. "I took one of my first rods down to Harry and Elsie Darbee's (the famous Catskill fly tyers) and they said they could sell them. One thing led to another and they kind of took me under their wing. They were incredibly well-connected people. They introduced me to everybody and sold my rods in their shop. So, when Leonard was sold I was contacted. There was no romance about it really, it was being in the right place at the right time." And as Carpenter soon found out about the profession of bamboo rodmaker, "It's basically loving it. It just takes you right over."

He moved back to Pennsylvania in 1990 where he now has a rod shop in the Fishing Creek Valley in the northeastern corner of the state, a great place for the trout fisherman as well as the rodbuilder.

There he crafts his well-known Browntone rods. He is also producing a classically styled trout reel called the Carpenter and Casey in two sizes. They have "S" handles with counterbalance and are constructed of aircraft aluminum and stainless steel. Both sizes have interchangeable spools and preset click drags.

Carpenter Browntone cane rods have been recognized as outstanding examples of the rodmaking art for many years. *Fortune* magazine chose them as "One Of The 100 Things America Does Best." Carpenter was one of only two individuals so chosen. Browntones take about fifty to seventy hours of handwork to make, and get their name from a lovely walnut coloring which contrasts beautifully with the golden colored nodes of the rods. The cane receives four coats of the finest tung oil varnish, and fittings are black anodized 18 percent nickel silver made by the rodmaker. Reel seat fillers are figured American black walnut, and guide wraps are mahogany with fine black tipping.

Carpenter rods are built of fifty-year-old Tonkin cane in two-piece models from 6-foot 3-inch to 7-foot 9-inch for line weights from 3 to 5, all with light to medium dry-fly (medium-fast) actions. A $7\frac{1}{2}$-foot three-piece model is made for a 4/5 line, also in a light dry-fly action. Prices are currently $1,500 for the two-piece rods and $1,750 for the three-piece. For the connoisseur as well as fisherman, Carpenter is also crafting a three-piece Mahogany model. It features a rich mahogany coloring with chestnut brown intermediate and primary wraps and fancy butt winds. The first guide is German agate, and fittings are oxidized nickel silver. Extra narrow hand-cut cork rings are used on the grip. Two-hundred-year-old mahogany is utilized for the slide band reel seat. Price is $3,800.

Carpenter's affinity for cane is obvious. "I love working with bamboo. It is an incredible material. It is so versatile. And I still think to this day that it enables the custom rodbuilder to make the very finest performing rod. I really like graphite, but as far as actually being able to take pieces of bamboo, to take an ideal and turn that into something that is functional—that's cane rods. And they are pretty."

As to the growing demand for good bamboo rods, Carpenter is still amazed at the fervor they create in anglers and collectors alike. "We aren't making fishing rods any more, we're building heirlooms and that kind of creates a paradox," he says. "I love casting them and I love fishing them. I didn't want them to be collectors' items." Spoken like a true fly fisherman and a true believer in the magic of cane.

Douglas Kulick of Fremont, California, has been a professional cane rodmaker since 1988 and has been working with bamboo since 1966. Kulick, by way of his company Kane Klassics, builds superb rods using the time-honored technique of hand planing the bamboo strips rather than tapering them in a milling machine. He also removes the inner apex of the tapered triangular strips, so when the sections are glued together it leaves a hollow rod which is lightweight but powerful.

Kulick has developed his own tapers, from traditional slow actions to medium and fast dry-fly ones. He tempers the bamboo to an amber color, then dips it in a polymer coating that resembles a traditional spar varnish.

Doug Kulick using the hand planing method.

Unique to Kane Klassics are Kulick's taper designs, which allow the construction of four- and five-piece bamboo pack rods from $5\frac{1}{2}$ feet to 9 feet for 3/4 to 6/7 weight lines. He also has multi-line fly rod sets with two butts and two tip sections to fish three different line weights. I have fished a $7\frac{1}{2}$-foot for 4-weight, four-piece model and it is one of the most delightful rods I have ever held in my hands. It has enough power to cover almost any trout fishing situation yet has a fine tip and fishes well in close. With a smooth progressive action, it is what an all-around trout rod ought to be. In addition, he makes one-piece fly rods from 5 feet and $6\frac{1}{2}$ feet and four spinning and bait-casting bamboo models.

Kulick feels that the saltwater market has been overlooked by most cane rodbuilders and is currently developing several rods aimed at flats fishing for bonefish, redfish, and even tarpon. He says they will be powerful yet lightweight enough to fish all day. Bamboo rods caught a lot of fish for Joe Brooks and other saltwater fly fishing pioneers, why not now?

Kulick fly rods are currently priced from $650 to $1,650; delivery time has averaged ten weeks over the last five years. Some of his rods are truly unique; some are real bargains. All are extremely well made.

Classic is a good word to describe the cane creations of Ron Kusse of Washington, New York. His rods are known for clean lines and elegant fittings matched with the very best in craftsmanship. A rodmaker for many years, Kusse is a former employee of Leonard, where he was a rodmaker and ran the Central Valley retail shop. In 1981 he decided that he would be much happier building rods under his own name. It was a good decision. Soon bamboo aficionados discovered his beautifully crafted rods and almost instantly he was backordered.

Bamboo rodmaking is Kusse's profession and he is serious about his product. "I make rods that are functional in casting as well as fishing; they stand the test of time. I never rush them," he says proudly.

He is a student of rod design and in tune with what his customers want, with fast-tipped light dry-fly rods being the current vogue. "I spend a lot of time on tapers. I make a lot of fast, quick rods and they cast as well and even better than graphite," he says with conviction. "You had fiberglass in the fifties and it wasn't very good, then you had graphite in the seventies and it got better and better and they began to cast better than cane rods, especially the old bamboo designs. But you have to say (as a rodmaker) that cane is a good material and because you can make it to perform the way you want, you shouldn't make old-fashioned rods. You should make cane rods to perform as well or better than a graphite.

"Graphite is good for casting long but not so good at casting short. The thing about cane rods is that they are good at eight feet. All my rods are tested between eight feet and a hundred feet. I like rods that will cast well at eight feet, will carry thirty-five feet of line, and then with a double haul will shoot it another seventy feet. It's a good rod when you can do that."

Standard Kusse cane rods are two-piece designs and have two tips with reel seats fashioned out of fancy hardwoods like black walnut, tiger-striped maple, and cherry. Fine knurled nickel silver slide bands or screw-locking reel seats and nickel silver ferrules can be ordered in either a black or bright finish.

Rods are built with a crisp dry-fly action in lengths from 6-foot to 8-foot for 3- through 7-weight lines. They are delivered with a brass-capped aluminum case and currently cost $1,045.

For a couple of hundred dollars more than the standard models a "mirror tip" rod is available with tips that are laid out so the nodes on each are identical. Thus the strength and action of each is an exact match to the other. A case with solid brass caps is included.

Kusse's top-of-the-line rod is called the Magnum Opus. He only

For every full-time rodmaker out there with an expensive brochure and a business card, there are perhaps a dozen or more that use the hand planing method to build a few rods per year. These rods, some of which are as nice as any you may see by the established makers, are fashioned for a few select customers or simply for friends and fishing acquaintances.

For the craftsman who wants to make his own rods there is an excellent book out called Handcrafting Bamboo Fly Rods (15315 Apple Avenue, Casnovia, MI 49318) *by rodbuilder Wayne Cattanach of Casnovia, Michigan. It comes in a useful ring binder complete with tapers displayed on charts and a computer disk for those so equipped.*

In addition there is a newsletter for rodmakers called The Planing Form (P.O. Box 365, Hastings, MI 49058), *which has a great deal of useful information for the builder using the time-honored hand planing method of rod construction.*

makes six per year and each is strictly custom designed in consultation with the customer. The price is $1,900 and up. For fans of four-sided rods the rodmaker also builds his great casting Quadrate in all three levels of trim. Recently he has brought back the ultimate midge rod, a classic Leonard taper called the Baby Catskill—a one-ounce, one-weight, six-foot bit of bamboo magic. Only a cane building wizard would attempt such a rod. The collectors should go wild.

If you are looking for a truly classic, magnificently crafted bamboo rod that will surely appreciate in dollar value and in your heart, then a Kusse cane creation is money in the bank.

A direct link to one of the past masters of bamboo lives along the Boardman River near Traverse City, Michigan. His name is Bob Summers. Thirty-eight years ago, at the age of 16, he began working for the great Michigan rodmaker Paul Young. The rods made by Young, who died in 1960, have attained a legendary status for their fine casting properties. In 1974 Summers started the R.W. Summers Rod Company in order to carry out some of his own ideas.

Summers makes rods that range from Midges, at $5\frac{1}{2}$-feet through $6\frac{1}{2}$-feet, to several trout models in 7-foot to 8-foot lengths. He also makes steelhead and salmon models up to an $8\frac{1}{2}$-foot rod for 8- or 9-weight line. His rods exhibit a semiparabolic action that offers a smooth casting action all the way into the grip. Even in very short lengths, these rods can cast an extremely long line, yet they are delicate enough for tiny flies and fine tippets.

I had heard about Bob Summers's line of rods for years, especially from my good friend Doug Truax who lives just a few miles from the Summers shop. This year I had the occasion to be in the Traverse City area and visited the rodmaker and casted a few of his rods. I was not prepared to be as totally impressed with them as I was. Every rod I tried—from a Midge to an $8\frac{1}{2}$-footer for an 8-weight that is Bob's personal striper rod—casted with

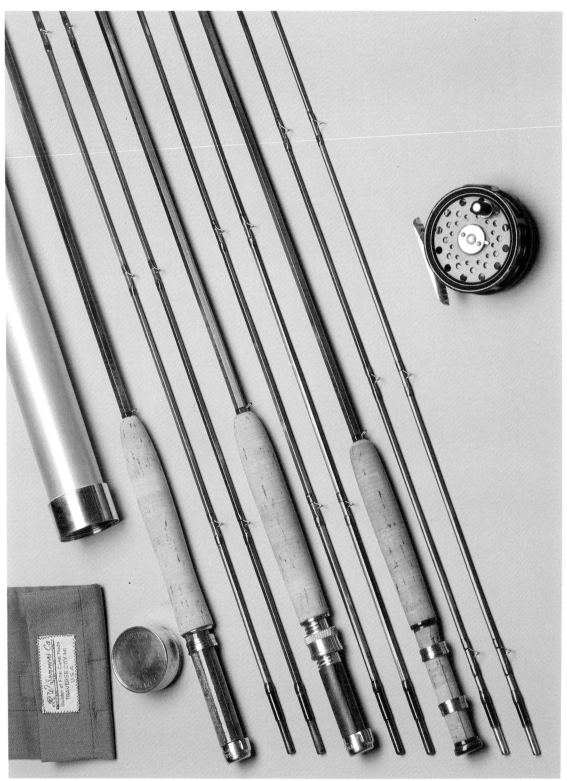

Bob Summers creates cane masterpieces, from his famous Midge rods for tiny streams to powerful salmon and saltwater models.

Bob Summers on the steps of his shop close to Michigan's Boardman River.

almost no effort, yet had tremendous power to throw a long line when needed. The tapers were superb. I immediately ordered a trout rod for myself. And it won't be the last.

The bamboo in a Summers rod resembles the same mottled flame tempering of a vintage Young. In addition to the cane, Summers makes all of his own rod components in his well-equipped machine shop, including reel seats, nickel silver ferrules, and his custom brass-capped rod tubes. At prices starting at $925 for a Midge, these surely must be the world's best bargain in cane rods. Delivery time is from eight months to a year.

Another rodmaker whose work falls into the bargain category is Art Weiler of Bound Brook, New Jersey. He hand planes exact reproductions of rods made by the late Everett Garrison. Garrison rods have achieved cult status among those who love and collect bamboo rods. And he is the patron saint for many rodmakers because he wrote the definitive work (Tom Moran calls it the *Koran*) on rodbuilding. His book, *A Master's Guide to Building a Bamboo Fly Rod*, was compiled by rodmaker Hoagy B. Carmichael after Garrison's death. It is used by many of today's limited-production makers as a basis for their work.

An original Garrison in good shape will fetch many thousands of dollars, but Weiler will make you a beautiful copy for $695 to $800. Each rod is built of hand-split and hand-straightened, aged Tonkin cane. Tempering and hand planing are done according to Garrison's methods. Weiler applies three coats of tung oil varnish and adds grips and fittings that are exact copies of Garrison's components. If you have ever hankered to fish with a Garrison, then Weiler will be happy to supply you one for little more than the cost of a couple of graphite rods.

Out West near some of our best trout fishing, excellent cane rods are being built under the name C.W. Jenkins in Aurora, Colorado. The man making the rods is Steve Jenkins, a second-generation maker who has taken over from his father Charles, a rodmaker of thirty years who is still active in the business as a consultant. Jenkins rods enjoy an enviable reputation with those who have been privileged to own and fish them.

I was first introduced to Jenkins rods by a friend of mine who saved his dimes and quarters and procured a 7-foot for 4-weight model. That was about a dozen years ago and he still loves and fishes the rod regularly. In fact he has, frankly, abused it a bit and it is still straight and casts well.

Presently Jenkins builds two- and three-piece rods with his traditional dry-fly action in 7-foot, 7½-foot, and 8-foot models for 3-, 4-, and 5-weight lines. The cane is offered in dark flamed, medium flamed and oven tempered (light). All have a cap-and-ring reel seat with hardwood spacer. Options like up- and downlocking reel seats, ferrule plugs, and tipped or custom wrappings are available. Jenkins's rods are very attractively priced at under a thousand dollars.

If you truly want a custom-made rod, and by that I mean almost anything you can think of in terms of taper, length, or line weight, Mike Clark of Lyons, Colorado, is your man. For over fifteen years he has been using the hand planing method of producing bamboo rods in his one-man shop. He offers one-, two-, and three-piece rods, with or without nodes, and they can be finished with tung oil or spar varnish, your choice. But, here's the kicker. You can order trout rods from 6 to 9 feet for 2- to 8-weight lines, salmon rods from 7 to 10 feet for 6- to 13-weight lines, or (get this) tarpon rods 8 to 11 feet for 7- to 13-weight lines (that's right, 13-weight). He also makes casting and spinning bamboo sticks and has several special signature fly rod models. Prices are $700 to $1,500 for fly rods and $600 to $1,000 for non-fly models. If you can think it up, Clark can make it.

R.D. "Bob" Taylor of Turners Falls, Massachusetts, has spent the past twenty-six years refining his craft. He worked for the Leonard Rod Company and Thomas & Thomas before turning his skills toward rods bearing his name. His standard rods come in two finishes: Flametone, a rich brown, and Natural, an

Summers in his Michigan workshop filing cane.

oven-tempered light straw in color. Both are wrapped in bronze/
gold with red tipping. Reel seats are applewood.

Taylor builds two- and three-piece models with medium
to fast actions. His Presentation Series rods have the look of the
old masters with a light, flamed Payne-type color, intermediate
wraps, handmade nickel silver fittings, and mahogany reel seats.
He also produces a limited series of cane salmon rods from an 8-

Engraved Daryll Whitehead rod and Saracione reel.

foot 6-inch for 7-weight line to a 9-foot 6-inch powerhouse for 9-weight line. Prices for his trout rods range from $1,300 to $1,950. Salmon rods are $1,400 to $1,550.

Daryll Whitehead of Seattle, Washington, is creating fine cane rods that are unique in the craft. Not only are they well executed and splendid examples of the rodmaker's art, but he is having the ferrules and reel seats engraved by Paolo Barbetti, a respected gun engraver.

Whitehead has always had a great admiration for the finely engraved guns he saw and loved in his father's gun shop as a boy.

When he began to fashion bamboo rods it was a natural extension of this interest to have the hardware of his rods so embellished. His rods are also set apart from others by their fittings, like fossilized ivory or cape buffalo horn reel seat spacers and ferrule plugs. They are correctly called "Deluxe" rods. Although this level of work costs more, each rod is sure to appreciate in value. As an added incentive to the connoisseur, Whitehead also offers matching Saracione reels engraved by Barbetti.

Joe Saracione resides in Sandy, Oregon, close to great steelhead and trout fishing. He is a custom reelmaker whose line of deluxe salmon, trout, and steelhead reels are some of the most exquisite ever made. Now he is gaining a similar reputation as a rodmaker.

Saracione's rods are designed to complement and perfectly match his reels. Medium dry-fly trout models range from a 6½-footer for 3-weight line to an 8-footer for 6-weight. Salmon and steelhead rods are medium to medium-fast semiparabolic, from an 8½-foot rod for 7-weight to a 14-foot spey rod for 10-weight line.

He flame tempers his rods in either a light or dark color, then adds 18 percent nickel silver fittings machined in his shop. The rosewood reel seats are precisely mortised, and the bamboo is beautifully varnished. Even the cases show incredible attention to detail. Rods and reels come in cases made of top-grain cowhide, oak tanned and hot stuffed with oils. Reel cases feature a suede-lined interior and are form-fitted to each size. For extra strength, the corner seams are French edged, and hand sewn with a double-needle lockstitch. Each rod case lid is blindstitched to give the cleanest look and to eliminate thread abrasion.

Joe Saracione's dual role as a reelmaker and rodmaker is unique in the history of fine fly fishing equipment. Prices are $1,350 for trout models and $1,500 for salmon rods. His semihollow spey rod retails for $1,750.

D.G. Schroeder of Janesville, Wisconsin, is an excellent custom rodmaker who builds his standard models in lengths from 6-foot to $8\frac{1}{2}$-foot in a medium-dark brown flame finish. All come with two tips, and feature burl walnut spacers in locking or cap-and-ring seats. Priced in the $925 to $975 range, they are a great value. Don also creates some gorgeous presentation rods with intermediate winds and special spliced wood and bamboo handles.

An old friend of mine, Steve Roche, has long since moved to the West Coast, but when we fished together in the Smoky Mountains over a dozen years ago, he expressed a growing infatuation with fly rods, especially those made of bamboo. We lost track of each other for quite a while, then, out of the blue, he called me this past year. He had given up his job as a psychologist and had become a full-time bamboo rodmaker. After he answered my trite question as to whether he ought to have his head examined, he said his company, called Stephen-Stuart, is producing a line of cane rods with tapers reminiscent of those devised by E.C. Powell early in this century, along with several new designs of his own. He is making fast dry-fly and medium trout actions, in addition to salmon-steelhead models. His Companion Series includes a two-tipped, two-piece rod with an additional butt section that is one foot shorter, making it a handy dry-fly rod. Roche also has a line of great-casting and handsome graphites. I know of no one who cares more about fly rods and fly fishing, and his rods are delightful and lovely casting instruments.

Rod companies have a long and rich history of turning out desirable cane rods, beginning with the H.L. Leonard Rod Company and continuing through today. Some of our most historic and treasured rods have been produced by such talent-laden consortiums. Actually, most companies have only one or two men who can be considered rodmakers, and sometimes their names are forgotten or the public's perception is that many hands produce their rods. Many times, other people at the company are simply going through a time-honored apprenticeship. It is unfortunate that these key rodbuilders' contributions to the art are not usually publicized.

The R.L. Winston Rod Co. has been at the forefront of bamboo rodmaking since 1929 when Robert Winther and Lew Stoner began calling their rods "Winstons." Since then a number of skilled craftsmen have made the company home, including Walter "Red" Loskot, Doug Merrick, Gary Howells, Tom Morgan, and currently, Glenn Brackett. Brackett, who has been at Winston since 1974, is the company's rod designer and maker. Although Winston began in San Francisco, it has been in the trout fishing town of Twin Bridges, Montana, since 1976.

Winston's varnished bamboo rods are a striking golden tan with luxurious nickel silver fittings. The company makes a complete line of thirty models, from light trout rods to steelhead and salmon models with their famous hollow-fluted construction. Prices range from $1,275 to $1,400.

Charles F. Orvis founded the company which bears his name in 1856 in the town of Manchester, Vermont, near the banks of the Battenkill River. A steady flow of bamboo rods

Don Schroeder's standard and presentation rods.

An example of one of the fine split-cane rods offered by the R.L. Winston Rod Company.

has come from its workshops ever since. In 1946 Orvis developed the world's first resin-impregnated rods, making them both water- and warp-proof. Those wonderful full-flexing dark brown sticks became favorites of Joe Brooks and Lee Wulff, who fished them all over the world. As a youngster, I remember looking at Orvis catalogs, dreaming of the day I would own a Battenkill cane rod. I still remember watching Joe Brooks on TV catching five- to eight-pound brook trout on his beloved Orvis bamboos.

I once owned a classic 7½-foot Superfine for 5-weight that was a wonderful trout rod. I wish I still had it. Today's models range from a small steam 7-footer for 3-weight to an all-around

8-footer for 6-weight. My favorite of the current rods is the Far-and-Fine model, a 7$\frac{1}{2}$-footer for 5-weight line.

For many years, Orvis rods were a rich dark mahogany in color; nowadays, they are more like a soft butterscotch. Battenkill models have two tips and the lower priced Madisons have one. Prices range from $600 to around $1,400.

A beautifully crafted Battenkill split-cane fly rod from Orvis.

Other rod companies, like England's House of Hardy, which still builds its historic Palakona split-bamboo rods, and the Powell Rod Company of Chico, California, now in its third generation of rodmaking (from E.C. Powell to son Walton Powell to son Press Powell), are reminders that fine craftsmanship and a sense of angling heritage are alive and well.

We are lucky indeed to have craftsmen who are still dedicated to producing split-bamboo rods. A fine cane rod seems like a living thing, delivering unmatched feel and the ultimate in fly casting pleasure. It is like an old friend, a faithful companion to be treasured forever.

FLY
REELS

Clockwise from top: Ballan, Saracione, Abel, Fin-Nor, Seamaster, and Pate Trout and Marlin fly reels. Several pictured are earlier models and are already highly collectible.

FLY
REELS

Gleaming gold, like a jewel in the searing Florida sun, a fly fisherman's reel gives up line to a giant tarpon crashing the shimmering flat. Meanwhile, half a world away, an Atlantic salmon, muscular and bright, fresh from the sea, fairly rips line from another angler's reel, testing it supremely in a cold Icelandic stream.

American fly fishermen have been on a frantic search for the last few years, joined by anglers from around the world. They are looking for the ultimate fly reel—a finely crafted, beautifully finished fishing instrument that will land the fish of their dreams and be a possession they are proud to own.

If you are among these faithful, count yourself lucky, extremely lucky, because you are living in a true renaissance period in the making of great fly reels. Never before has there been such an array of finely crafted, well-designed reels available to trout, salmon, and saltwater anglers.

Over the past one hundred years there has always been a great variety of fly reels to choose from for trout and bass fishing. In most cases all a reel had to do was hold the fly line, and perhaps a few yards of backing, with enough tension to keep the spool from over-running if a fish ran a short distance. Thus grew the old notion that a fly reel is "just a place to store line." Salmon anglers normally used bigger versions of trout reels that held more line and backing, and hoped the fish they hooked would not run too far. Some well-heeled anglers, if they fished the big-fish rivers of Canada and Norway, used expensive Vom Hofes, Hardys, Zwargs, and Leonards, but their numbers were few.

It was after World War II that a small group of American fly fishermen began to crave something better. With the war over and the world returning to normal, a new fly fishing frontier was singing a siren's song—the ocean. Adventuresome anglers became convinced that anything that swam could be taken on a slender rod and a feather-and-hair imitation. Tarpon and bone–fish were fair game as well as deepwater bruisers like tuna and amberjack. Even sailfish and marlin were quarry to be taken on a fly rod.

The myth that a fly reel's purpose was only to hold line was gone forever. We began to realize that the fly reel was not the least important part of our gear. When you are casting to a fish that can run out backing the length of a couple of football fields in a few seconds, the reel becomes the most important piece of equipment.

A big-fish reel must have three qualities: It should hold enough backing for the largest fish you may encounter; it should be sturdy with fine tolerances to take the punishment and stress from fighting huge fish; and most critical, it should have a reliable drag. The drag should be not only strong enough to pres-

Tycoon/Fin-Nor gold anodized fly reels, like this current model, have been a standard of the industry for many years.

sure a big fish but must be smooth to protect the tippet when a fish is tearing around with a great deal of line out. There also should be little or no start-up torque to overcome when the fish stops and then starts another run.

All of these qualities are necessary in a reel for fly fishermen who tackle the strongest saltwater fish and the largest salmon. It is true that many remarkable catches have been made on standard off-the-shelf reels and even inexpensive mass-produced models, but it is also true that they might fail at the worst possible time.

Our finest reels have always come from individual craftsmen and companies dedicated to producing the finest product regardless of cost. These fishing tools are machined from the best quality alloys of aluminum, stainless steel, and bronze. Most are made in limited numbers. Demand for some far outstrips production, while others are available immediately. A few of these reels are entirely handmade while others are crafted on computer-driven milling machines. However they are manufactured, there has been an explosion in the last few years in the number of elegantly crafted, essentially handmade fly reels. Most are single-action (there is one notable exception), and many are available in your choice of direct-drive or anti-reverse. There are more than a dozen reelmakers producing these ultra-quality reels. Most seem to be doing well with their offerings despite some expert opinions that the market is too small for this many makers.

Perhaps it is a bigger market than earlier naysayers thought. There are more anglers turning to the pleasures of fly fishing than ever before. There is also a movement in this country back to craftsmanship and the intrinsic value of items that are well made. It is pride of ownership that draws us to these reels. Our time spent afield is more precious than ever, and it just makes one feel good to own and use something that is exceptionally well made. Many of these handmade reels are already sporting collectibles.

To be sure, becoming the proud owner of one of these reels can be expensive. Many models sell from $300 to well over $1,500. That is a fair amount of money for a reel. Or is it? It seems everything is expensive today. Is an imported compact car really worth $20,000? Is a pair of hunting boots really worth $150? That is what some cost these days, even though they will wear out and be yesterday's news in a couple of years. A finely made fly reel, on the other hand, should last at least 25 years. Even at $500 that's only $20 a year for the pleasure of owning and using the very best. That's really not too bad when you consider that a couple of movie tickets with popcorn and drinks costs more than that.

Why are there suddenly so many reelmakers? There are probably several reasons. In reality, a number of reels on the market today have been in the planning stages for quite some time. Perhaps they have surfaced because the time seemed right. Many makers decided to build their own reels because of slow or non-existent delivery from established makers and, more important, they felt they could build a better product in the spirit of good old-fashioned inventiveness.

Whatever the reasons today's reelmakers have for their designs, they owe a debt of gratitude to the pioneers of the modern-day, finely crafted big-fish fly reel: Bob McChristian of Miami, Florida; and Stanley Bogdan of Nashua, New Hampshire.

Their handmade reels, produced 1,500 miles apart, have become symbols of excellence to fly fishermen around the world. From Norway to Australia, from Costa Rica to Iceland, the fastest and strongest of fish are sought by fly fishermen with their cherished Seamasters and Bogdans. The makers' clientele might be at times a bit different; a tweed-clad earl or duke fishing a Bogdan on a misty Scottish salmon beat is quite a dissimilar sight from a heavily tanned Florida Keys guide poling a bonefish flat with a brace of Seamasters ready for action. However, both of these anglers share the same love for a product that is finely made, beautifully finished, and mechanically superior.

Those are the attributes Bob McChristian was looking for when the first Seamaster fly reel came off the bench forty years ago. A stocky, powerfully built man still going strong at eighty-two years old, he has retired from the business and turned production over to his thirty-year-old grandson, Robbie Jansen. (Bob plans to remain active in the design of Seamasters and will be the perfect sounding board for Robbie.) Hurricane Andrew destroyed their shop and a goodly amount of machinery, but they have moved into new quarters, and Seamasters are back in full production. Those beautiful gold and black anodized reels are being delivered once again.

If you are new to fly fishing or have been stuck in Timbuktu for an extended period of time let me fill you in on Seamaster fly reels. Made as close to perfection as human hands can muster, the reels incorporate thoughtful design and the kind of ruggedness that will withstand years of hard use. They keep on working through the most difficult tests that saltwater fly fishermen can give them (for decades). Indeed, Seamaster reels are treasured by those who own them. You won't see them checked in with the luggage for trips to faraway destinations. Everyone I know who owns one carries it by hand along with his other valuables.

Seamasters are built slowly and precisely, which explains why fishermen years ago had to wait many months, even years, for delivery. Though nothing is changed in the way the reels are made, Robbie tells me that most future orders will be filled within three weeks to nine months, depending on the model ordered. If even that seems like a long time, remember: the moment you unpack your new Seamaster, its value on the secondary market will probably be a couple of times more than you paid for it.

Before he started the company, McChristian had used a lot of reels that just didn't cut it.

"I fished hard, I fished for big fish, and I fished often," he says, remembering those early days. "For big fish you need eight to nine pounds of drag, and everything I tried didn't hold up."

McChristian knew then exactly what it would take to create a reel equal to the tasks saltwater fly fishermen are assigning their equipment these days. Marlin, sailfish, tuna, and other powerful oceanbred adversaries are pursued with the fly. A number of saltwater fly fishing fanatics are presently engaged in the quest of the first two-hundred-pound tarpon. Many of these folks come to Seamaster for their reels.

A leading south Florida light tackle pioneer, Bob has been involved in fishing professionally since 1935, when he became a charter boat captain at the age of twenty-three. In 1946 he opened a tackle shop called Capt. Mack's Tackle Shack and has been known to Miami area fishermen as Capt. Mack or just Mack ever since. Always an innovator, he has produced fine fishing products for many years. When he found that big, toothy tropic fish made short work of plastic topwater chugging lures, he decided to make his own out of cedar. These lures had a heavy wire running the length of the bait to keep the hooks from pulling out. He called the plug the "chuggitt" and although he no longer produces them, very similar

Seamaster frames and spools are precisely milled from solid aircraft quality aluminum. Anodizing protects the reel from saltwater corrosion. This anti-reverse Tarpon model is no longer made and is a much sought-after reel on the secondary market.

commercial plugs are used all over the world today with great success.

From 1955 to 1964, Mack made what is perhaps the most exquisite spinning reel ever produced. Tired of the spinning reels not holding up, he machined one out of solid aluminum alloy, stainless steel, and bronze. Deeply anodized on the outside, it was as beautiful as it was rugged. The world had not seen a spinning reel like it before and likely never will again. The examples I have seen were made in a finely polished gold or blue anodized finish. Untold marlin, sailfish, tarpon, tuna and giant grouper were caught on those reels. On the front cover of Mack's old brochure a prominent Miami angler is shown with five Pacific marlin caught on the reel with fifteen-pound-test line in a single day. On the back cover a fisherman is shown with a 120-pound white marlin caught on a fifteen-pound line on a Seamaster spinning reel and another angler is pictured with a 107-pound grouper caught on twelve-pound line.

Unfortunately, because of the many hours of machining, hand fitting, and polishing involved in the spinning reel, it eventually became too costly to produce. Those lucky anglers still possessing one have one of the most finely crafted pieces of angling tackle ever produced.

In that early Seamaster brochure, which also included such things as a custom made gimbal rod belt, a spinning reel line winder, and a spinning rod roller guide set, McChristian had a single page set aside for his Seamaster fly reel. Only one type was offered, an anti-reverse slip-clutch model. That was the reel that secured a place for the name Seamaster in angling history. According to McChristian it was the first fly reel on the market designed specifically for saltwater use. That's also the reason a fisherman ordering one of his reels today gets a Seamaster instead of a McChristian. "I wanted to tie my products in with the sea," says Mack of his company's name.

Seamaster Dual-Modes work as an anti-reverse reel when the fish is taking out line so the handle remains stationary, and as a direct drive when reeling in for more control over the fish.

It is just that dedication to his saltwater fly fishing clientele that has endeared Bob McChristian to his customers. They know he delivers a product made carefully and exactly, backed up with a great deal of experience and knowledge of saltwater fly fishing. Only a few short years ago, before the current explosion in hand-made reels, Mack estimated that Seamasters had caught 90 percent of all saltwater fly fishing world records over fifty pounds. A list of McChristian's customers reads like a list of *Who's Who* of saltwater fly fishing. Mack has sold reels to anglers not only in the United States but in Australia, Japan, Africa, Saudi Arabia, France, England, Sweden, Switzerland, and a number of other places, making them a truly international commodity.

The reason Seamasters are so highly praised is simple. They are made as well as is humanly possible. "Each reel is built à la carte," McChristian says proudly. "Every customer's reel is built expressly for him."

He feels strongly about his reels and why they are held in such high esteem. When asked why they are so good, Mack says, "it's simplicity in design, dedication to the smallest detail, and hand fitting."

With an average of ten or more hours of work in each reel, it takes six days a week and many nights to keep up with orders. The word handmade takes on a new meaning when you see a Seamaster up close for the first time. It is an imposing piece of craftsmanship. Though lightweight for its tremendous line capacity, it is also incredibly strong. Machined out of solid aluminum bar stock with key components made of stainless steel, the reel's smoothness of operation seems unreal for its massive strength. Disengage one of Mack's direct models from the drag and give it a spin. It seems like it's never going to stop, thanks to sealed precision ball bearings.

From that first anti-reverse model, the Seamaster line grew to three slip-clutch reels and five sizes of direct drive. The anti-reverse models were called the Salmon, Tarpon, and the Marlin,

Bob McChristian putting together one of his famous Seamasters.

obviously for the fish they were designed to catch. Those models are now discontinued and are among the most sought-after reels on the collector market today.

Why so many sizes and different reel types? McChristian felt that to be considered a complete company he had to make as many models as possible to fulfill customers' needs. He was also thinking of his customers' safety when he brought out his first anti-reverse fly reel. That was back in the days when saltwater fly fishing was just starting to gain in popularity. Many people were trying it for the first time, sometimes with fish as big or bigger than they were. Mack felt that was a potentially dangerous situation.

"When a big tarpon is in midair, then makes a fast run and a novice gets excited and grabs the handle of a direct-drive reel he can get injured," the reelmaker points out.

However, direct-drive Seamasters have been the choice of many experienced anglers and experts, especially in the larger sizes. I have always preferred direct drives because when you turn the handle on a direct drive, line has to come in, giving more control over the fish. The handle and therefore the spool can be locked, which is helpful when pumping up large fish from the depths. This can shorten the fight. The longer a fish is on the higher the chance that something can go wrong or the tippet will fatigue and break. Seamaster direct drives also have been out of production for a while but Robbie promises to bring them back in the near future, at attractive prices.

The current series of Seamasters, introduced a number of years ago, are called the Dual-Modes. These are essentially anti-reverse reels when the fish is taking out line, yet act as a direct drive when you are reeling. Dual-Modes come in Mark II, Mark III, Marlin One, and Marlin Two models. There is also a Masterpiece series, a limited edition set of engraved Mark II and Mark III Dual-Modes with Bob McChristian's signature and issue number on the back. All gold anodized, they are exquisite. They come in a walnut case and sell for $4,000 a set.

Like all things considered wonderful, standard Seamaster reels are not cheap, with the Dual-Modes currently ranging from $1,150 to $1,500. But then, price is a relative thing. If you paid a handsome sum for a classic sports car and it gave you many years of pleasure and faithful service, yet you knew that at any time you could sell it for more than you paid for it, you would surely consider it one of the best bargains of your life.

Perhaps the most outstanding feature of a Seamaster reel is its superb drag. The primary component is a single piece of high density cork, which has a secret formula filler added to solidify the material and increase compressibility and friction. These drags have stood the test of time. Besides being extremely fade resistant they have what McChristian calls "no breakaway torque." That means once the drag is set on a particular poundage, it will stay there even if the fish makes a blistering run from a dead stop. There is no extra starting force to overcome. That can make a difference when a big fish is tearing around on a fragile tippet.

To prove this, McChristian has a demonstration. He will tie the line on the reel to a scale nailed to the ceiling of his shop. Next he sets the drag until it pulls eight or ten pounds and then pulls line off the reel slowly with an occasional jerk downward to imitate the sudden surge of a fish. The needle on the scale stays exactly where it is.

The most visible feature of Seamasters is their gorgeous deep anodized gold finish. One of the most handsome to be seen on any reel, it is tough and seemingly impervious to salt water.

Traditionally the reels had a two-piece frame held together by stainless-steel pillars. Now they feature a one-piece frame machined out of aluminum bar stock. Other key parts are made of stainless steel.

Regardless of what they are made of, or what they cost, one thing is sure, if you are lucky enough to own one you belong to a exclusive fraternity, or as Capt. Mack refers to it, his "family" of knowledgeable and discriminating customers.

For more than half a century Stanley Bogdan of Nashua, New Hampshire, has been making the finest salmon and trout reels in the world. Although his reels are sometimes used by customers in salt water, it is the Atlantic salmon for which his reels were designed. On rivers around the world where the biggest salmon are taken, like Canada's Restigouche and Grand Cascapedia and Norway's Alta, Bogdans are the reel of choice. Stan, along with his son Steve, makes nine traditional 2.1 multiplying wide-spool salmon reels, as well as a half dozen 1:1 ratio reels for trout and steelhead. The salmon reels are also available in 1:1 ratio, and all models can be ordered in right- or left-handed retrieve. Bogdans are without a doubt the most famous and desired freshwater reels on the planet. They have achieved a cult status with fly fishermen willing to wait years for delivery. Priced from about $1,100 to $1,500 they certainly are on the high end of the scale, but like Seamasters no one ever loses any money on a Bogdan. Their worth on the secondary market is as strong as ever.

Although most salmon and trout fishermen have heard of these exquisite creations milled out of solid aluminum alloy bar stock, many don't know who Stan Bogdan is or even if he exists. Most of the people in the midsized New England town where he lives and works don't know who he is either. That includes many of his neighbors. Well, he does exist. He remains hard at work and looks twenty years younger than his seventy-four years.

He still produces the line of reels that have become legends on salmon rivers all over the world. At many of the finest salmon clubs on the most famous streams it is considered almost in bad taste to fish with anything other than a Bogdan. Using something else is akin to being invited to hunt bobwhite quail on a posh south Georgia plantation and showing up with a rusty J.C. Higgins pump shotgun.

Although his reels and the name Bogdan will certainly have an exalted place in the history of fly fishing, Stanley Bogdan remains "just old Stan" to his friends and neighbors. He is personable, with a quick dry wit, and the very epitome of the Yankee craftsman. With a sharp New England accent and the glint of far-off leaping salmon in his eye he reflects on the reels he began producing fifty-one years ago.

"I really don't know why I started making them," the craftsman says, "I guess it was my machinist training and a love of fishing. My first love is salmon fishing. I prefer to do it more than anything else in the world."

Indeed, fly fishing for Atlantic salmon is a very important part of Bogdan's life. He does it as much as he can, and he has been invited to fish some of the finest rivers in the world by affluent customers who appreciate his work. When invited into Bogdan's home for a visit and talk of reels and fishing, the lucky visitor will probably be offered a bit of smoked salmon. Whether caught by Stan himself or one of his customers, it will certainly

*One of the most intricate and time-proven drag systems is seen on Bogdan
salmon reels, which are constructed like a fine watch.*

be served with the reverence reserved for the finest of game fish.

Although the reels Bogdan builds have a very traditional
look with lightly gold anodized aluminum frame, black anodized sideplates, and S-curve counterbalanced handle, they were
his own design from the start.

"I didn't dare look at the competition, so as not to copy,"
he remembers. "I never took another reel apart."

Bogdan has had a long history of designing reels. Anyone
today who fishes with the popular Orvis CFO is using a reel that
was a prototype in the Bogdan shop two decades ago.

Of all the attributes of a Bogdan reel, the ten-position drag is far and away the most important. When a twenty-pound salmon is streaking across a pool and precise pressure has to be exerted on the fish to stop it before it gets to a falls or rapids, a smooth, strong drag is paramount. Bogdan reels are up to such a task.

I know, because a number of years ago while fishing Iceland's Laxa i Adaldal, I hooked a tremendous salmon while casting from an island in the river. The twenty-five-pound cockfish, which we found out later was the largest salmon caught in that country that year, took off back to the North Atlantic with me stranded on the island. I managed to get to the main shoreline of the river, but by that time the fish had ripped off over 150 yards of backing from my Bogdan reel. As the salmon took more and more line out I was able to increase the drag in small, precise increments. I'll always believe the Bogdan reel made the difference in landing that fish.

The drag mechanism on the salmon models is a wonder of design and craftsmanship.

"It's just like the mechanical brake on an old car," Stan explains. "Two brake shoes (Delrin) are pushed against a drum. It has fine adjustments in ten positions, which come from a cam and coil springs."

The drag pressure can be set from very light to heavy by pushing a little lever into different notches on the sideplate opposite the handle. As the lever is pushed forward, the cam exerts more pressure on the brake shoe. While a fish is on, the angler can change his drag pressure instantly from a couple of ounces to several pounds, as the situation warrants.

When all of this is added to a gearing system that makes for a 2:1 retrieve ratio on some models, it would seem rather complicated and tough to keep up with. It would for the average fellow, but not Stan Bogdan. Don't ask him how many parts are in a reel, because his tongue-in-cheek answer will be, "I don't really know, I'm afraid to check."

Bogdan salmon (top) and trout reels are the most sought-after freshwater reels in the world. They are crafted in a wide variety of sizes to cover almost any angling situation.

Don't believe him, because Bogdan knows where every piece to every model goes, its precise measurements, and exactly how they are fitted together. Until recent years, this vast store of information was all in Bogdan's head. Now after fifty years there are blueprints, which must be a great relief to Steve Bogdan, who will be making the reels when Stan retires and goes fishing.

A trip to the Bogdan shop is an experience. Instead of the latest computer controlled milling machines found in many reelmakers' shops, these angling masterpieces are handmade, as Stan puts it, "on a bunch of junk." Originally costing a grand total of $440, all of the machinery appears to have been away from the factory of its origin for a very long time. Bogdan obviously takes great pleasure in telling visitors, with a bit of devilment in his voice, "It's just the same stuff we started with."

Why not use the most modern tools to produce his reels? He can only explain it as "just plain stubbornness."

With particular pride, Bogdan points out his favorite machine—his eleven-dollar drill press. The press itself cost six dollars and the used washing machine motor to run it another five bucks.

"Just call it Yankee ingenuity," Bogdan laughs. Evidently this mishmash of ancient machines, most of which is older than Steve, is capable of doing what Stan asks of it, because the product speaks for itself.

Because of what it takes to build a handmade reel, each individual unit requires at least fifteen hours of work to complete. However, one thing that Stan has never shied away from is work.

"It's all handwork, that's the only way to do it," he says. "I'll be damned if I'll cut corners."

The truth of that statement becomes obvious when you closely examine a Bogdan reel. Beautifully finished, it works with a smoothness that could pace your heart. There are reels for almost every fly fishing situation: four trout models, two steelhead, a grilse/sea trout version, and nine salmon sizes. There is also a Signature series to commemorate his fifty years of building reels.

With so many models, and demand at an all-time high, Bogdan is reluctant to give delivery times. Like Seamasters, it all depends on which model the customer orders and when it comes up on the work rotation. Be forewarned it will take awhile.

"In about a year," Bogdan tells his eager customers. "I just don't tell them which year."

About a decade ago Stan finally broke down and started making his trout models. "I had to," he laughs, "so many people in the New York area wanted one. They threatened me with bodily harm. Then it took me three years to convince myself."

The demand for these trout reels became so high several years ago that some were being bought at auction for four and five times their cost from the maker. Before Steve came to the shop, Stan spent eighty hours a week, year in and year out, building reels. Today Stan is taking more time off to fish.

Although people like the Duke of Wellington and the Duke of Marlboro use Bogdans on their private salmon beats, there are plenty of

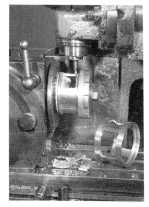

Bogdan one-piece frames start out as a solid piece of aluminum bar stock.

Stan Bogdan assembling a perforated-spool trout reel in his Nashua, New Hampshire, shop.

everyday folks using them on eastern trout streams and western steelhead rivers. Whether they are used on the Restigouche, the Grand Cascapedia, the Alta, or the Miramichi, or on the Yellowstone, the Beaverkill, or a favorite No Name Creek, Bogdan reels will always be admired, cherished, and fished with pride by discriminating anglers across the globe.

In south Florida another reelmaker has developed a loyal following with hard-fishing and astute anglers. There is pride in the man's eyes. It is backed by confidence in a product well made and thoughtfully designed. He has no doubts about his brain-child: it is crafted as skillfully as his hands can make it and will serve well for a very long time. His fondest wish is to produce something that his customers will enjoy using and that will endure. He has.

The man's name is Ted Juracsik, a tool and die maker from Oakland Park, Florida. He is presently producing some of the finest fly reels ever to see action on a tarpon flat or salmon stream. Co-designed with the well-known international angler Billy Pate, they are called the Billy Pate Reels by Ted Juracsik.

He is justifiably proud of his work. Pates are one of the most trusted fly reels among the hard-to-please Florida tarpon guides who must depend on their equipment for their livelihood. There are three reasons why Juracsik reels are so highly praised.

The first, and perhaps most important, is credibility. These reels were designed by fishermen, for fishermen. Billy Pate is an internationally respected angler who knows what it takes to catch fish with fly tackle. He has taken more than a dozen saltwater world records on fly tackle with the Pate-Juracsik reel.

Ted Juracsik is also an avid and skilled fly fisherman whose free time finds him chasing tarpon or redfish in Florida Bay, bone–fish in Biscayne Bay, or permit out of Key West. With such an input of skill and experience going into the design of the Pate-Juracsik reels, little wonder they are considered one of the most well-thought-out fishing instruments in angling history.

Ted Juracsik is an avid fly fisherman who constantly tests his creations in salt water's unforgiving environment.

The other two reasons the Pate-Juracsik reels are unique result from Ted's training as a consummate machinist. Since the reel's inception, all major parts have been designed to fit corresponding parts on any other reel model. Should a part wear out or break in years to come, a replacement can be ordered from the maker. This was unheard of in the limited-production hand-made reel market. Usually a reel must be sent back to the manufacturer for a new part to be made and fitted. This feature must be credited to Juracsik's hard work. Once the reel's design was established, he went to great expense and effort to meticulously make a die for every major part in the reel.

The amount of work it required paid off and assured the third reason for the reel's ever-growing acceptance: availability. You can actually get one! Instead of a wait of one or two years—even more with some reels—the reels are sometimes in stock for immediate delivery. They are made assembly-line fashion by Ted and a group of highly trained machinists in his shop, which speeds up production without sacrificing the quality or workmanship.

Juracsik reels are made in five sizes in anti-reverse or direct drive and are named for the fish they are designed to catch. The smallest is the Trout (it is my favorite Alaska reel), the Salmon (I have one I treasure because I caught a bonefish on its maiden cast), the Bonefish (a great size for large bones, permit, or general big-water fishing), the Tarpon (obviously for the silver king), and the Marlin (a huge reel that is a super reel for giant tarpon, tuna, sailfish, and marlin). All models are available in gold and black or all black anodized.

In order to understand why Pate-Juracsik reels enjoy such a high reputation and popularity, one must understand not only how they originated and evolved, but how Juracsik thinks as a craftsman. His demands for quality are fostered from an Old World education taught during a traditional four-year apprenticeship as a tool and die maker in his native Hungary. In 1957 he was forced to leave the country of his birth after a turbulent year of fighting the Russians during the invasion and revolution. Twenty-one years old at the time, he immigrated to America to establish a new life.

After spending a year in a Brooklyn orphanage, Juracsik began to work in his chosen profession and eventually developed

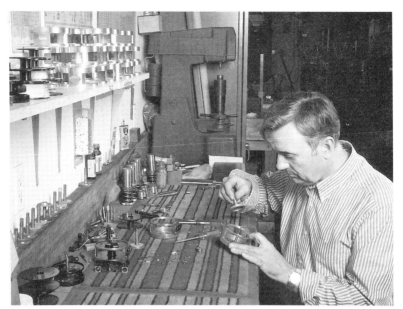

Ted Juracsik building his Billy Pate fly reel—one of the reels most trusted by saltwater fly fishing guides and sportsmen.

a successful tool and die business on Long Island. With his career secure, he found time to fish—something he had always loved. As a boy he had played hooky from school to fish in the Danube River. Now on Long Island he turned to striped bass fishing, invariably accompanied by one or more of his wife's seven brothers. Vacation trips to south Florida taught him what powerful, fast game fish could do to inferior tackle. His training as a skilled machinist quite naturally led him to upgrading tackle for himself and friends, and he started making handmade manual bails for spinning reels and solid spools for Ambassador casting reels.

It was during one of Juracsik's trips to Florida that he met Billy Pate, the owner of a prominent tackle shop in the Keys. Pate had been thinking about designing his own reel for some time, both to use and to make available to his customers.

Billy Pate still fishes all over the world with that first reel, along with several others, in his quest for another world record tarpon. And he's been rough on them. "My reels go into my boat in March and are fished constantly until July with no maintenance, no cleaning, just fishing," Pate says with pride.

That same sense of pride is visible in Ted Juracsik's eyes when he talks about his reels.

"I enjoy people fishing with something I made and having them tell me they are not having any problems," Juracsik says with a small trace of an accent. "You must make sure reels work forever. Fifteen years later parts should fit. When someone buys my reel he is making a lifetime investment. I was taught as an apprentice in Hungary that when you make something, you make it right."

It is appropriate that the Juracsik-Pate reels were put into production in 1976, the year of the Bicentennial. What better time than the celebration of America's two hundred years of freedom for an immigrant, like so many before him, to start making an improved handcrafted product and take advantage of the free enterprise system? Production of the Juracsik reels has come from the same spirit of building a better mousetrap that has always fueled the aspiration of inventors and craftsmen wishing to excel.

The first reels were an anti-reverse design where the handle remains stationary as line is pulled off the spool. In 1980 a direct-drive model was added to the line. All models are corrosion proof. Nonferrous parts are bronze, brass, aluminum, Teflon, and cork. Everything else is stainless steel. The one-piece frame and spool are machined from heat-treated aluminum and designed so that the spool reinforces the frame, making it almost impervious to shock. To prove it, Juracsik takes a demonstrator reel and drops it about four feet onto a concrete floor.

"You see," Ted points out with a grin, "the frame just can't be bent even when you accidentally drop it on a hard surface."

The large diameter cork drag is another special feature. "Material for the drag must be soft and compressible but of the right consistency," Juracsik maintains. "The drag must gradually take over, not all at once, with no start-up torque to overcome."

Other features that make the reels exceptional are double anti-reverse dogs for fail-safe anti-reverse and double clickers which produce two different sounds so a guide can tell if his client is gaining or losing line. An oil-impregnated bushing is used around the main gear which weeps out oil when it gets hot during an extended battle. The hotter the gear gets, the more oil is emitted, thus eliminating the necessity of lubricating that important part.

Little details like the handle knob and the drag control wheel add up to sound design. The drag knob is large in diameter and knurled so it can be easily controlled with fingers that may have suntan lotion and sweat on them. The drag also tightens the same way you are reeling so it doesn't increase when the fisherman doesn't want it to. A longer handle shaped to fit a fisherman's fingers gets knuckles away from the spool and lessens fatigue while providing better control. These are but a few of the attributes that make Juracsik-Pate reels the thinking man's reel.

Each is a labor of love. To show a profit, Juracsik has been careful about their evolution, producing them with a consistent level of excellence. "My father told me the old proverb I live by, 'Only stretch as long as your bed covers. If you don't, your feet will get cold.' "

Juracsik's reels carry a lifetime guarantee on parts and workmanship. The guarantee even covers parts that need to be replaced due to normal wear. When he delivers a reel to a customer, he tells the person not to take the reel apart or clean it—other than washing it off after use in salt water—for a period of several seasons.

"Just fish it hard and tell me what you think of it in a couple of years."

Joe Saracione of Sandy, Oregon, is producing a Deluxe Series of trout and salmon reels with split bamboo fly rods to match each reel—something that to my knowledge has never been done before by a single craftsmen.

When I first put my hands on a Deluxe reel, it struck me that I was holding one of the most exquisite pieces of fly fishing equipment I'd ever seen.

Deluxe reels are made in nine sizes, from a tiny $2\frac{1}{2}$-inch midge reel up to a $4\frac{1}{2}$-inch model for big salmon. They are styled in the tradition of the classic reels of Edward Vom Hofe. Trout models have a preset gear and pawl, while salmon and steelhead reels feature both the gear and pawl, along with lever-action, oil-impregnated cork drags.

These serpentine-handled beauties are constructed of stainless steel (side bands, knobs, and cross pillars), aluminum, bronze, and nickel silver. Instead of ebonite or hard rubber for the sideplates, Saracione is using black delrin, which is almost indestructible. The fit and finish is as good as any reel ever made.

The impregnated cork drag on the larger reels is lever controlled with positive intermediate stops and can be adjusted throughout its range by a simple turn of a screwdriver.

These reels are not inexpensive—from $765 to $1,315. An engraved presentation model is also available at a higher price. All reels come in a beautiful, matched size hard-leather case. Saracione's delivery times have lengthened in the last year due to increased demand, but if you are patient you can have one in less than a year. He promises to bring out a new line of saltwater reels in the near future.

For the past several years, Steve Abel's fly reels have taken the market by the throat and said: "This is what fly fishermen have been wanting all along." From trout streams to blue water, Abel's eight models have been used successfully all over the world. They range from the tiny O Model for 2-, 3-, and 4-weight lines to the giant 5 Model which takes a 12-weight line and 880 yards (over one-half mile) of thirty-pound backing. These disc drag reels are beautifully machined out of high quality aluminum and are available in a glossy or flat black anodized finish.

Joe Saracione Deluxe trout reel with one of his handmade bamboo fly rods.

Abel spent three years developing his new TR/Series of simple trout and salmon reels. They are fully machined and finished in the Abel tradition. Designed to take line weights from 2 to 8, they are made from aircraft aluminum and stainless steel bar stock. The three models—TR/1, TR/2, and TR/3—weigh from 3.9 to 4.5 ounces. They feature a high-gloss finish, counterbalance, rapid release spool, rim control and pawl-click drag, and easy left-right wind conversion. These reels are bound to be as successful as their original disc drag counterparts.

Gold anodized fly reels from the grand old south Florida firm of Tycoon/Fin-Nor were one of the first great designs for big-game fishing. They have been modified and changed over the years, but a complete redesign a couple of years ago brought dramatic improvements. Offered in direct drive and anti-reverse, the new Fin-Nors feature a one-piece frame and spool machined from bar-stock aluminum. Their anodized finish is either traditional deep gold or gloss black. The rim control spool is perforated and rotates on oversized stainless steel ball bearings. Drag comes from a large cork disk and has an outgoing line click. Changeover from left to right is easy. A new 4.5 reel, built with a large diameter spool for fast line pickup, is perfect for tarpon or sailfish.

Fin-Nor has introduced a line of lightweight reels for freshwater and light saltwater fishing. Called the Fin-Ites, the reels feature a single direction bearing system with a smooth disc drag for both fine tippets and big-running fish. They have rim control and quick-change spools which convert for right to left retrieve in seconds. Their one-piece housing and spools are machined, and the drag adjustment knob has detents for precise settings. Fin-Ite reels have a deep anodized finish.

Bob Corsetti of Nashua, New Hampshire, builds reels with the correct name—Peerless. His trout, steelhead, and salmon reels are styled in the Edward Vom Hofe tradition and reflect precision hand-craftsmanship. They feature S-curve handles with ma-

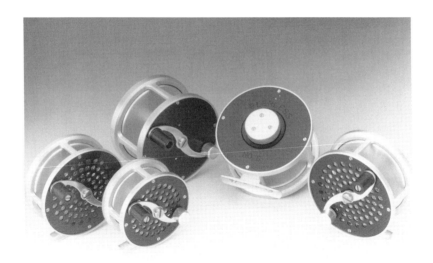

Bob Corsetti's traditionally styled reels come in a number of trout and salmon sizes with solid and perforated spools.

chined aluminum spools and frames. Trout models have perforated spools, while those on salmon reels are solid.

Trout reels come in Nos. 1, 1½, 2, and 3. All have oil-impregnated bronze bearings and a stainless steel bearing shaft that is centerless (straight) ground for smoothness. Each is black and clear anodized for a durable, corrosion-resistant, non-glare finish. The adjustable drag system on the trout models is a unique pawl design that can be easily switched from right- to left-hand retrieve. The click is ultra-smooth.

A new model this past year, the Model 1½ has an adjustable drag knob. The reel measures three inches in diameter, weighs 4.9 ounces, and holds a 5-weight line with thirty yards of backing.

Also new are the No. 5 and 6 salmon and steelhead reels. They have a modified and improved drag system similar to the famous reels of Vom Hofe. In addition, each salmon reel has an adjustable pawl drag to prevent free spooling when set on extremely light.

All Peerless reels are beautifully made and reasonably priced. Most comparable reels cost twice to several times as much.

Ted Godfrey of Reistertown, Maryland, has been making excellent custom salmon and steelhead reels for some time, and now has improved their performance even more. The reels are all-new inside and out. Six salmon models are available. Built with a classic serpentine-handle multiplying design, they feature a large drum drag system with a ten-position drag and adjustment lever. Retrieve ratio on the salmon reels is 1.9:1 for fast take-up of the line. The spool can be changed without any loose parts to misplace, and the drag setting can be adjusted with the turn of a screw. These handmade reels cost between $700 and $750 and should provide a lifetime of reliable use.

W.A. (Bill) Adams of West Haven, Connecticut, is custom building a traditional trout reel in two sizes. The reel has an S-shaped handle and a silver and black anodized finish that resembles the look and feel of classic reels, but with several differences. For one thing, the design is patented. Features include rim control, a pleasant sounding adjustable click drag that is easily reversible, quick spool release lever, and a uniquely designed handle and knob assembly that is extremely strong. The reels are available in sizes $2\frac{3}{4}$-inch diameter and 3-inch diameter for 5- and 7-weight lines. Both are very light, $3\frac{5}{8}$ ounces and $4\frac{3}{8}$ ounces, respectively. The reels retail for $335.

Bill Ballan is making classic trout and salmon reels at his Carmans River Reel Company in Bayport, New York. The Trout Classic is a raised pillar design that has a traditional look that fits in just right on any fine bamboo rod. It is made in three sizes, the Midge, the Baby Trout, and the Large Trout. They have a fixed drag and counterbalanced S-curve handles.

Heirloom Classic models have a one-piece frame, and S-curved handles with counterbalance; they come in two sizes. Both reels have a choice of perforated or nonperforated front plate. Prices are extremely reasonable and workmanship is excellent.

Bill Ballan reels like this beautifully made steelhead model are also available in trout and salmon versions.

Ballan has also recently unveiled a salmon reel in three sizes which will add to an already fine group of products.

    Charlton Outdoor Technologies is a new company run by Jack Charlton, who has designed a series of reels that could be the benchmark of the future. He makes models in four different diameters that take several widths of spools, making the line capacities just right for everything from trout to blue water. All feature a unique, large, hand-filling drag knob, perforated spools, light cage frame, and sealed drag that is waterproof. The anodized aluminum can be had in either a glossy or matte finish. As an addition on some models you may have your name engraved on the drag knob.

Perhaps his most renowned reel is the SST, which is his top-of-the-line reel, made entirely of titanium. Prices currently run from just over $230 to $3,600 for the largest size titanium reel.

Many other reelmakers are coming and going with each new season. Some will make great reels that will stand the test of time; others will fail. Whether they do or not, it remains true that never before in history have we seen such an array of fine fly fishing instruments.

FLIES

Saltwater flies and bass bugs tied by Greg Snyder, Billy Munn, and Jim Stewart.

FLIES

Dancing on the crystalline surface of a New York trout stream, a Quill Gordon dry fly, beautifully tied in the Catskill style, entices a rising brown trout. Riding the swift, tannin-colored waters of an Icelandic river, a Green High-lander feather-winged Atlantic salmon fly attracts an outsized specimen of *Sulmo salar*, the prince of fishes. Chugging the tepid surface of a lily-pad-filled Southern pond, a deer hair bass bug, exactly imitating a tasty frog, awaits the explosive strike of a fat-bellied largemouth bass. Swimming seductively through the co-balt waters of the Pacific, a bright yellow and blue streamer darts and flashes in search of a sailfish, tuna, or some other saltwater heavyweight.

Imitations of various fish foods, expertly crafted of feathers and hair and tied on a hook, have been fooling fish for many centuries. The ancient Egyptians fished with rods as long ago as 2000 B.C. and the Macedonians, it is generally believed, used artificial flies to catch fish about A.D 200. But it was Dame Juliana Berners, an English nun who first penned fly fishing instructions in her famous *A Treatyse of Fysshynge With an Angle* in 1496, and who started the English-speaking masses thinking they might have a bit of fun *fly* fishing.

Although much has been written about other equipment, for the fly fisherman it is the fly which is the most important element in the equation. If a particular fly isn't what the fish wants, everything else is academic. More time has probably been spent devising flies for the various fishes we pursue across the globe than in all of our other exercises in the name of angling sport.

Undoubtedly the highest form of artistic expression in fly tying is seen in the full-dress feather-wing patterns for Atlantic salmon. One of the great achievements of angling history, they were a product of the far-reaching explorations of English travelers during the height of the British Empire in the early nineteenth century. These intricate and difficult-to-tie flies sometimes contain as many as thirty different beautiful materials, extracted from birds from distant locations. Many of the feathers came from the Orient, Asia, and Africa. Exotic birds like Indian jungle cock, peacock, and crow were used, as well as guinea fowl and ostrich from Africa, silver and golden pheasant, Egyptian goose, blue macaw from Latin America, and even feathers from the blue jay.

Those wonderful building blocks were then taken by tyers from England, Ireland, and Scotland and transformed into bright creations aimed at the capture of *Salmo salar*. Their names even reflected their high place in the hearts of anglers, with such de-

Paul Schmookler's Black Argus Variation is an example of the very best in feather-wing Atlantic salmon flies.

Paul Schmookler at his fly tying bench with an outsized example of his work.

lightful designations as Jock Scott, Silver Doctor, Black Dose, Green Highlander, Thunder and Lightning, Blue Charm, Pink Lady, and Lady Caroline.

Because salmon were generally the quarry of well-heeled gentry and royalty (although the art of the poacher should not be overlooked), salmon flies not only saw use in Great Britain but also in such faraway angling beats as the Arctic rivers of Norway and the great streams of northeastern North America. They have always been expensive compared to trout flies because of the difficulty in tying them (a single fly can take from several hours to weeks to complete) and because those affluent patrons who admired and fished with them were willing and able to pay an artist's fee for their manufacture.

Many patterns were developed according to the whims of

British tyers and were designed to work well on particular streams or to please their patrons. These flies are impressionistic and are not meant to imitate anything specific. Salmon do not eat during their spawning run back to the river of their birth, so there are several theories as to why they take a fly. Some think it is their memory of food, either insects or minnows, from when they were voracious parr. Others believe it is the striking reflex that they fine-tune for survival in the ocean. Whatever the case, the basic theory for choosing a pattern is, dark flies for dark days and bright flies for bright days.

That was certainly the case for the flies selected by my gillies on trips to Iceland, Norway, and Ireland. My grandest salmon ever, a heavy shouldered twenty-five-pound hook-jawed male taken in Iceland's Laxa i Adaldal was enticed by a featherwing Black Doctor tied by a local guide. The fish struck late in the evening as the Arctic sun bathed the Kinnarfjoll mountains in a wash of rose. Dark day, dark fly. That wonderful, if rather crudely tied deceiver, rests in a place of honor, stuck into the band of my favorite fishing hat.

Salmon flies hold such a fascination for anglers that they command the same reverence and expressions of esteem that are usually reserved for bamboo rods, handmade fly reels, close companions, and lovers. In Ireland when we discussed fly preferences, the gillies would describe particular selections as "lovely" or "brilliant" while the rest of our equipment was relegated to the station of mere tools.

A modern day tyer who creates "brilliant" flies is Paul Schmookler of Millis, Massachusetts. He is considered one of the very best full-dress salmon fly tyers in the world. He began to collect materials for his art over twenty-five years ago as a world-traveling professional entomological collector of butterflies and other insects. Through his travels he began to acquire a love of beautiful feathers. Already an exceptional trout fly tyer, he soon discovered the ultimate destiny for his feathers in the form of salmon flies. Although he ties classic patterns, his artistic interpretations of what a salmon fly can be have to be seen to be believed. They are masterpieces, awash with brilliant colors in a symphony of feathers that have the flow and spirit of a well-executed painting. He has taken the art of the salmon fly to heights that a nineteenth-century British tyer could have only dreamed about.

If you desire such a fly you may have one, but with a price tag that is more commonly connected to museum-quality paintings than a fishing lure. Suffice it to say a Schmookler fly will cost from hundreds to thousands of dollars. Obviously they generally go to affluent and discriminating collectors of fishing equipment. To own a specimen puts one in very select company.

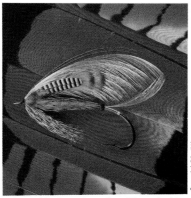
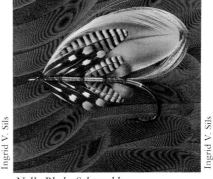

Schmookler's artistry is evident in his Chatterer pattern.

Nelly Bly by Schmookler.

Bob Veverka of Underhill, Vermont, is a superlative fly tyer in several classical schools. He crafts not only lovely feather-wing salmon flies but landlocked salmon streamers and steelhead spey patterns as well. If a Grey Ghost or Yellow Badger is your fancy, he is the man to see. A commercial tyer since 1980, Veverka has traveled extensively to share techniques and patterns with other creators of fine flies. His steelhead flies go to anglers in Oregon, Washington, and British Columbia. Hairwing, spey, and tube Atlantic salmon flies from his vise are used in Canada, Norway, Iceland, and Russia. For his saltwater customers, he ties for striper

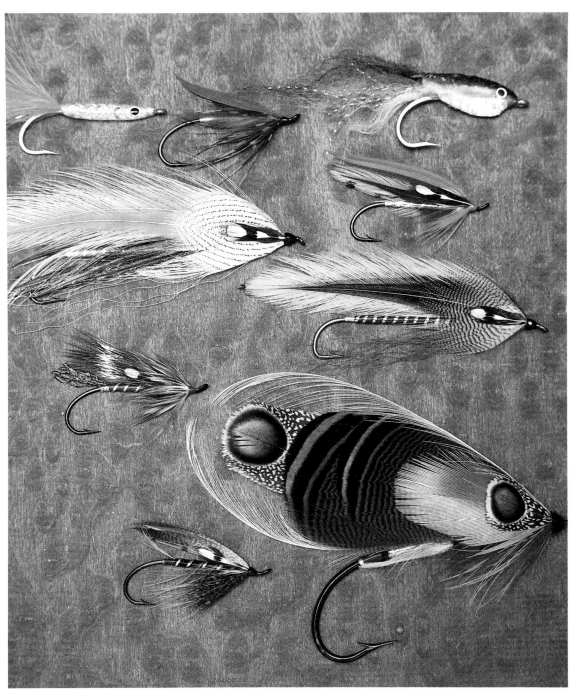

Bob Veverka flies are masterpieces, whether they are salmon, trout, or saltwater patterns.

enthusiasts in the Northeast, and tarpon, bonefish, and permit anglers fishing southern locations.

A fine teacher who conducts classes on salmon fly construction, his flies have been on display at several museums and featured in a number of books. His prices range for three dollars for a standard fishing fly to ten dollars for a salmon spey pattern. Landlocked salmon streamers are currently $25, and a full-dressed featherwing is $100 or more. Classic flies from a classical tyer.

For the tradition-minded trout fisherman, no other fly has the magic of a well-tied dry fly. That is especially true of an imitation of an adult mayfly from the Catskill school of tying. These flies are appreciated for their economy of materials and delicate proportions. They were born on the streams of the Catskill Mountains in New York: the Neversink, Beaverkill, Delaware, Willowemoc, Esopus, and Schoharie rivers.

The heritage of the Catskill dry fly can be traced to near the turn of the century when the native brook trout of the eastern mountains were beginning to disappear because of their gullibility and lack of compatibility with civilization's water-warming byproducts. Luckily, in the 1880s the brown trout had been introduced from Germany and Scotland, and this more hardy and selective fish was beginning to take a strong hold in the streams formerly full of brook trout. Because of the brown's taste for aquatic insects that were hatching on the stream, unlike the brookie's wanton strikes at anything that resembled food, new, more imitative flies were necessary.

Enter a slim, reclusive fisherman by the name of Theodore Gordon, who is known as the father of American dry-fly fishing. He devotedly fished the Catskills, and particularly the Neversink River, from the late 1800s to the early 1900s. A studious type, he noticed nature in its finest details and discovered that brown trout knew exactly what kind of mayfly was hatching and preferred to eat accordingly. No gaudy attractor patterns for them. Gordon made it his business to know the same. He found that hatches of insects could be predicted and therefore matched. The dry flies he came up with, and those developed by later tyers, were tied sparsely with great attention to the proper color, silhouette, and variegation of body and wings. His most famous fly is the Quill Gordon, designed to imitate the dun of a large mayfly that is the first significant trout food to emerge on eastern streams in the spring.

Many famous and innovative fly tyers from the region followed: Herman Christian, Ed Hewitt, Roy Steenrod, Rube Cross, William Chandler, Walt and Winnie Dette, Harry and Elsie Darbee, and Art Flick. They all added new patterns and continued to tie dry flies in the Catskill style. Wonderful names like the Hendrickson, March Brown, Light Cahill, and Blue-winged Olive became part of our fly fishing vocabulary. Since then many thousands of different and effective dry flies have been developed across North America including those satisfactory for the demanding trout fishing of our western Rockies. However, it is the Catskill dry fly that remains the most eloquent expression of the dry-fly tyer's art.

Del Mazza of Utica, New York, a consummate fly tyer for more than thirty-five years, ties in the best traditions of the Catskill school. From his bench come exquisitely proportioned mayfly counterfeits, both for the fisherman and the connoisseur of the classic dry fly. His accolades from knowledgeable fly fishermen speak volumes as to why he is one of our generation's most respected tyers.

Bill Hunter, who is a tackle and travel consultant and himself a superb salmon fly tyer, says about Mazza's work, "The visual proportions are perfect. The symmetry is ideal. His flies are neat and clean and precise. Del is one of the best tyers in the country."

Nick Lyons, well-known author and book publisher, is also among the many fans of Mazza. "Del's flies are meticulous, bril-

Del Mazza at his bench in Utica, New York.

liantly constructed, and eminently fishable. I treasure those I own," he says.

I agree. And despite the status he has achieved in his profession as one of its very finest craftsmen, Mazza is also one of the nicest men you will ever have the pleasure to deal with. The ghosts of past Catskill masters would be proud.

About the same time that Theodore Gordon was wading the Neversink, the black bass found its own champion, Dr. James Alexander Henshall. In 1881 he wrote the seminal work on fishing for the "green trout" entitled *Book of the Black Bass*. He had found a grand fish that was readily available to more fishermen across the country than any other and as he put it, "I consider him inch for inch and pound for pound the gamest fish that swims." In his book he wrote of fly fishing with bugs made of deer hair, which made the flies extremely buoyant and lifelike to the bass. They just looked good on the water. It was an era far removed from the electronic fish finders, 200-horsepower motors, and 70-mph bass boats of today's overglamorized professional fishing tournaments. It was a time of lazy summer afternoons and relaxing fishing, casting "bugs" to likely looking spots in search of a hungry bass.

Fly fishing for bass began to wane with the popularization of first the bait casting reel and, after World War II, the spinning reel, which made it possible for anyone to fish effectively. It was a sport that lay dormant until recent years when fly tying innovators like Dave Whitlock, Larry Dahlberg, and hair bug tying genius Tim England inspired a new generation of fly fishermen to enjoy the pursuit of the black bass. These tyers' creations of mice, frogs, minnows, grasshoppers, leeches, and crawdads made of deer hair and many other hair and fur materials are truly inspirations to make any bass angler take up his fly rod and head to the lily pads and stump fields. The common bug or streamer has been given a face-lift.

Jim Stewart of Tampa, Florida, is a virtuoso hair bug tyer. His love of the fly rod and bass fishing has led him to develop some incredible hair creations. They are gorgeous. Because he has found a way to pack the deer hair more tightly than most tyers, he can actually carve the body of his bugs into any shape he desires, including those of some classic wooden bass lures, like the Lucky 13 and the Dalton Special.

Quill Gordon by Mazza.

Adams by Mazza.

Isonychia Quill by Mazza.

Hendrickson spinner by Mazza.

His professional training as an architect stands him in good stead for crafting and designing bugs that involve the difficulty of incorporating four different colors of hair.

His portfolio of flies is entertaining to look at and deadly to largemouths and smallmouths. Some of my favorites are: Stewart's Buzz Bug, which has a spinner at the front of the fly to gurgle when stripped, with a purple- and green-striped body with oversized eyes; and Stewart's Jointed Popper—a deer hair body of purple, blue, and black, with a jointed tail of blue, purple, white, black rubber hackle over light blue, teal blue, and purple grizzly hackles. The head is a fluorescent rose. Sounds like something good to eat doesn't it? Stewart's Spin-N-Jim is shaped like a small sunfish and has a brown, tan, black, and fluorescent orange body with a spinner behind and rubber hackle trailing.

He ties a couple of great frog patterns—one that looks like a green and yellow Hula Popper and the other like a popular topwater frog/spoon. And for classic lure fans, his Stewart's Lucky Wiggler is trimmed to look and dive like a Lucky 13. Its body is constructed of chartreuse, white, and orange hair.

Stewart's flies might be considered a bit costly at around $10 each on average, but since they take at least an hour to tie, they are worth it and should make any bass proud to have been caught with them. And he does want his customers to fish with them, although he realizes many end up on display.

His favorite story about using his flies, he tells with a laugh. "Two Christmases ago I gave one of my close friends several flies for a present. When I asked later that spring if he had caught anything on them he replied, 'Oh no, I wouldn't *use* them, they have a place of honor on the mantel over my fireplace.' Well, I fixed him this past Christmas. I gave him several more flies but they arrived in a ziplocked bag, packed in a combination of water, tobacco, cigarette ashes, and mud from my backyard. You should have heard him yell! After he got them washed off he began to fish them and has caught a number of nice bass. But he

Jim Stewart's fantastic deer hair bass bugs.

has warned me never to do that again."

Texas is a good place for trophy largemouth bass, and a great place to get superlatively tied bass bugs. Billy Munn of Bridgeport, Texas, has been tying frogs, sliders, sculpin, moths, minnows, and other bass tidbits for nearly thirty years. A postal employee who ties part time, he has won many honors for his beautifully crafted bugs. An active member of the Federation of Fly Fishers, he won their Buz Buszek Memorial Fly Tying Award in 1986 for his significant contributions to the sport. His other awards include the Texas Flyfisher of the Year (1984), FFF Southern Council Fly Tyer of the Year (1985), and several awards from the Fort Worth Flyfishers.

He has taught many fly tying classes at the FFF national conclaves held in West Yellowstone, Montana, as well as at conventions in Arkansas and Texas. An admirer of Dave Whitlock's bass flies, Munn's workmanship is on a par with anyone tying with deer hair. He also creates excellent McCrab permit flies.

After World War II another frontier began to beckon to fly fishermen—the trackless ocean. In the crystal clear water of ocean flats, and the deep blue depths offshore, swam fish of such power, size, speed, and beauty, they were beyond the imagination of most freshwater fly fishermen. On the flats, the bonefish, a muscular, torpedo-shaped sprinter, became a primary target. Pioneers like Joe Brooks proved to us that they would take a properly presented fly.

The bonefish is roughly equivalent to a trout or bass in size. Even a two-pound fish is big enough to be fun, and a five-pounder is an excellent catch. If you manage to land a ten-pounder, you have a superb angling trophy. Anything over that is world class, a reason for church bells ringing and your picture in the paper. It is said that a bonefish can race one hundred yards in three seconds! No trout or bass can match that explosive first run.

The other star of the flats was the tarpon, the giant silver king whose powerful runs are measured in hundreds of yards and tremendous heart-stopping leaps. Later, fly fishermen began to match their wits and tackle with toothy barracuda, snook, and the most neurotic fish that swims, the permit. Farther north, anglers began to chase inshore fish like the bluefish and striper that lived in bays and harbors. A darling of today's inshore fly fisherman is the redfish or channel bass.

Ultimately fly angling explorers began to look to the giant warriors of blue water—the sailfish, tuna, and marlin—for new conquests. Fishing innovators like Dr. Webster Robinson proved to us that such fish, too, could be caught on the slender rod. Writers like Lee Wulff made us think we, too, could catch them. Large sharks, brilliantly colored dolphin, and even the phenomenally powerful and fast tuna became fair game. The jet plane made it possible to reach faraway fishing destinations in a matter of hours. If it swam in salt water, it was now a fly fishing target.

The field of saltwater fly tying is one filled with brightly colored materials and unlimited imagination for new and more successful patterns. Neon-bright colors of hair and feathers, and flashy silver mylar that would scare the begeebers out of a brown trout, are magnets for slashing strikes from saltwater bruisers. For the flats, imitations of shrimp and crabs take on new and more innovative forms with each passing season. For deeper water new baitfish-sized attractor patterns are being created. Even squid are the subject of mimicking fly tyers. With the burgeoning popularity of saltwater fly fishing, the best is yet to come.

From the unlikely location of Phoenix, Arizona, Greg Snyder is tying expertly finished saltwater flies. He currently offers 185 different pattern and color choices for everything from bonefish to marlin from his business called King Neptune's Flies. How did a guy living in the desert become a leading saltwater fly tyer? Well, for one thing, as he points out, it is only three hundred miles to the Sea of Cortez from where he lives, so he can regularly try out his new creations. He was born and raised in Portland, Oregon, and began fishing in the 1960s on the Wilson River. In 1973 he moved close to Del Cooper, a well-known northeastern fly tyer. Cooper helped him through the embryonic stages of learning to tie and soon Snyder was tying commercially.

When he moved to Arizona to work for a turbine engine company he shelved his tying for several years, but after seeing an article in a fly fishing magazine about the Sea of Cortez he became interested in saltwater flies. With the tremendous growth in saltwater fly fishing, he decided it was time to get back to the bench. He soon became acquainted with notable fly fishing experts, including Lefty Kreh, Jack Samson, and Dan Byford, and used their experiences as well as his own to begin developing patterns that would prove successful. He finds the big offshore patterns for marlin, sailfish, wahoo, and tuna to be the most challenging because density, profile, and size are so important. Snyder

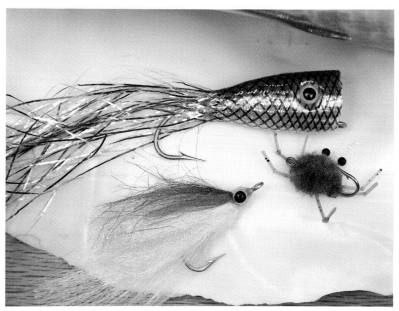

Greg Snyder flies will catch a variety of saltwater game fish.

Billy Munn deer hair bass bugs, and saltwater and trout flies.

ties for several retail outlets and is now also manufacturing cus-
tom-tied saltwater leader systems. I have seen many of his flies
and have very successfully used a number of them on the flats.
They work, and are tied with great care and workmanship.

With the boom in tying all kinds of flies, there are scores of
excellent tyers around the country today. Some have been at it
for dozens of years and others are unknown. The artists on the
preceding pages are representative of the many others who are
creating masterpieces in fur and feathers.

Craig Brown's wooden fly boxes are an elegant and practical way to protect valuable flies.

FLY BOXES & NETS

If a trout is to be caught there must be trout flies. If there are flies there must be fly boxes. And if the trout is to be landed there should be a landing net. For the finest of those accessories the fly fisherman may look to the state of Michigan. Over the last year I have been hearing rumors from several sources of a fabulous netmaker living in that northern province. Now I find there are two such craftsmen, both doing extraordinary work and living not too far from each other: Craig Brown of Elk Rapids, and Ron Reinhold of Williamsburg.

A woodworker since 1981, Craig Brown is a self-taught craftsman who began as a furniture maker and a designer of com-

Craig Brown creates a variety of nets and boxes for the fly fisherman.

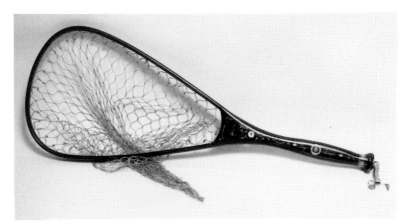

Ron Reinhold net created for Trout Unlimited to present to President George Bush has extensive carvings and inlays and the President's official cuff links set into the handle.

mercial/residential woodwork. He has been concentrating full time on exhibition-quality wooden boxes for jewelry since 1986, and then, more recently, boxes for fishing flies. They have been sold internationally at more than seventy galleries. Made entirely of woods like mahogany, walnut, cherry, and lacewood, they even have wood hinges and lid supports. Inlays and catches are of various rosewoods or ebonies. A more elegant resting place for treasured trout and salmon flies is hard to imagine.

His nets, made of ash or hickory for strength, are extremely sturdy, and real beauties with their intricate multiple inlays of exotic woods. They reflect superb wood-crafting skill and have a lovely flawless finish. He also makes a fly tying chest, which he is currently refining, and will be crafting several new products in the near future, such as a five-drawer salmon fly box, a gun cleaning kit, and several new net designs. His prices are very reasonable considering the craftsmanship, with boxes priced at $140 to $180 and nets at $140 to $275.

Ron Reinhold is, as the Richard Oliver auction house calls him, "the recognized world's premier maker of collector quality wooden landing nets." He makes some truly remarkable nets that are certainly the most highly crafted ever built. To understand his quest toward the upper limits in the design of a wooden landing net, you need go no further than reading his business card. It says, "Ron Reinhold—Entrepreneur Unextraordinare. Your single source for: Harebrained Ideas, Dead-end Inventions, Time Mismanagement, Non-Profit Investments, Some Decent Nets, Staffs, Releases, Books, Do-It-Yourself Stuff, Etc., Etc." Intriguing to say the least.

Actually, Reinhold does have his hand in all of those subjects, but for anglers, it is his nets that command the most attention. That is especially true of his elaborate collector nets like the one he made for Trout Unlimited to present to President George Bush. Its description follows: Made of beautiful deep-stained curly maple, it has 200 inches of twelve-karat gold wire twisted and inlaid as a double border paralleling the cord groove. An additional 50 inches of gold wire is wrapped at the junction of a deer antler cap. The front of the handle has a relief carved brown trout with inlaid scroll work, inlaid moose-antler diamonds, and the President's own personal cuff links inlaid with his signature in brass wire. On the back side is a life-sized relief carved grasshopper, caddis fly, carved feather overlaid with

Reinhold's remarkable nets reflect a great deal of workmanship to please the user or collector.

a jungle cock feather, carved opposing mayfly spinners, and inlays of moose antler and wood similar to the other side. A remarkable piece of work, it has a value of $5,000.

Of course not all of Reinhold's nets are quite that ornate. They can be had for as little as a couple of hundred dollars, but his average specimen with a bit of carving and such will run about $500. He has worked with many conservation organizations like Ducks Unlimited, Trout Unlimited, and so on, with his nets to date bringing in over $250,000 to those associations. For the connoisseur of fine angling accessories, a Reinhold net is an ultimate possession.

HANDMADE
KNIVES

Folding knives by (from top) Ron Lake, Frank Centofante, Jess Horn, Henry Frank, Harvey McBurnette, and Steve Hoel.

HANDMADE
KNIVES

Knifemaking is man's oldest craft. Its practitioners have been valued by kings and and paupers, by soldiers and sportsmen.

The custom knifemakers practicing their ancient craft in the United States today are producing knives that are at once tough tools, fine art, and museum pieces. We are presently enjoying one of the greatest revivals in the art and craftsmanship of knifemaking in the last five hundred years. After an awakening in the late 1960s and early 1970s, and a period of tremendous growth in the 1980s, custom knifemaking is enjoying a true renaissance in the 1990s. Craftsmen have discovered that the knife is not only a reliable and well-made tool but a canvas for the showcasing of their artistic talents. Knifemaking has come of age.

Everybody needs a good knife. Since cavemen fashioned pieces of flint and obsidian into cutting instruments for hunting and warfare, we have always depended upon and admired a well-made knife. It became the most useful tool that the world has ever seen, an essential part of life.

Because of the renewed interest in custom knives, the Knifemakers Guild was formed in 1970 by a group of eleven craftsmen dedicated to promoting custom knives and ensuring that good business practices were followed by its members. The Guild, which now has more than four hundred members, has become an internationally respected organization and a benchmark for all such groups.

In 1976, the year of our Bicentennial celebration, the American Bladesmith Society was formed "to preserve and promote the art of bladesmithing." The Society's membership, which also now numbers over four hundred, is at the forefront of the hottest movement in knifemaking, the forging of high-carbon tool steel and Damascus (pattern welded steel) into useful and beautiful knives.

There are two groups of knifemaking craftsmen, each with different methods and philosophies. Those who use the *stock removal* method take a piece of alloy steel and essentially grind everything away that doesn't look like a knife; those who use the *forging* method utilize the age-old method of fire and hammer.

In the forging method (bladesmithing), a craftsman takes a piece of high-carbon tool steel, heats it in a forge, and then hammers it into shape to realign and tighten its molecules until the metal has greater density and strength. The steel is then tempered by heat until it has the best qualities of hardness and toughness. In a well-executed blade the hardest steel will be at the cutting edge for maximum sharpness while the back will be progressively softer for toughness. The handle or tang will be softer for resistance to breakage.

Damascus is created when, using the same methods of the ancient swordmakers and knifemakers of the Middle East, two different kinds of steel are welded together, one low carbon and the other high carbon. Once the weld is completed, the steel is drawn out by hammering, folded, and welded again, with the procedure repeated until the optimum number of layers (300-500) is attained. The resulting blade is said to possess the best qualities of both steels: toughness, resiliency, edge-holding ability, and ease of sharpening. After the metal is forged it is etched lightly with acid to make the different steels contrast in height and color, giving it an unsurpassed richness. It glows with character and beauty. Some bladesmiths claim Damascus is the best of all knife steels, while other knifemakers argue that it is inferior to modern tool steel. All agree, however, that it is the most beautiful of steels.

To be accepted into the American Bladesmith Society, a knifemaker must complete the requirements of first an apprentice smith, then a journeyman smith, and ultimately a master smith. They must learn to make knives that excel in cutting, chopping, and bending tests. For example, a journeyman smith must forge a blade that can cut a hanging one-inch hemp rope about six inches from the loose end, completely severing the rope in one stroke. After that, the same knife must then cut a 2x4 board in two at least twice, then be capable of shaving hair from the applicant's arm! Subsequently the blade is clamped in a vise and bent at least 90 degrees without breaking. A knife that survives that gauntlet demonstrates why the proponents of forging believe their knives are the best. A master smith must also forge a traditional pattern welded Damascus blade that will pass the same tests.

On the other hand, 90 percent of all handmade knives today are built by the stock removal method using high-speed belt grinders to work sophisticated alloy steels. Most stock removal makers assert that for a "using" knife, there is no way a forged tool steel or Damascus knife can perform as well as one made of a modern sophisticated alloy. These steels contain elements such as carbon, manganese, molybdenum, vanadium, and tungsten. Not only do they have great edge-holding ability, but fantastic resistance to abrasion. Their sharpness will last and last. In addition, modern steels like ATS-34 or 154-CM are almost entirely rust and stain resistant, unlike tool steel or Damascus.

These metals are too difficult to machine in a factory, so they must be ground and finished by hand. While an average factory knife might be good for skinning one or two deer before it needs sharpening, knives made of these steels can be used on five, ten, or more deer.

American custom knifemaking can trace its heritage through the innovative and pioneering spirit of four men: William Scagel, Bo Randall, Bob Loveless, and Bill Moran.

Bill Scagel, an eccentric from the backwoods of Michigan, can be considered the father of modern custom knifemaking. From about 1920 until his death in 1963 he made knives that were decidedly superior to the store-bought variety. American sportsmen had not yet gotten over the mystique of the big bowie knife, but Scagel made smaller and more useful knives that felt better in the hand and performed their tasks more efficiently. His knives were also quite attractive, with unique leather and stag handles and a curved knife emblem stamped on the blade. They are treasured and valuable collectibles today.

Bo Randall, an Orlando, Florida, citrus grower, began making knives in 1937 after seeing a Scagel in use. He was so impressed that he decided to make his own knives. From that day until the present, the "Randall Made" logo has achieved legendary status. During World War II, Randall knives were carried by many servicemen who needed a optimum blade on which they could stake their lives. They have been used and trusted by astronauts in the unforgiving environment of outer space. On the game fields of the world, countless sportsmen have praised

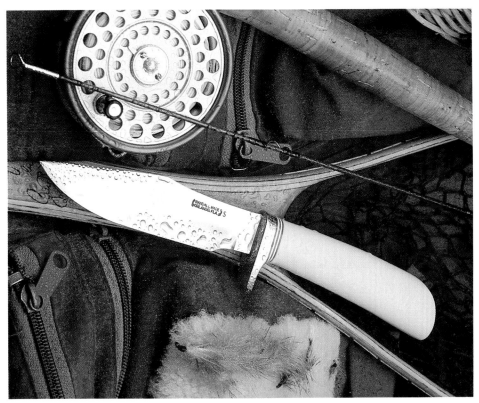

Randall trout and bird knife.

Classic Bo Randall hunting knife with leather handle.

Randalls for their edge-holding abilities. Most of the custom makers who were building knives in the 1960s and early 1970s used Randalls as a basis for their designs. Today "Randall Made" knives are still produced in Randall's shop in Orlando, Florida, now under the direction of Bo's son, Gary.

Bob Loveless of Riverside, California, has influenced more present-day knifemakers than any other individual. In 1953 when he tried to purchase a Randall from Abercrombie & Fitch and was told he would have to wait several months, Loveless decided to build his own. That started a career that has changed our concept of what a using knife should be. Instead of the heavy five-, six-, or seven-inch blades that were prevalent in those days, Loveless made his hunting knives with thinner blades of four inches or less. He also dropped the point of his hunters, which is much more practical than the upswept pointed knives of that period.

Corbet Sigman folder is an example of the highest craftsmanship in knifemaking.

Damascus skinner by Don Fogg, fighter by Tommy Lee, and forged period rifleman's knife by Daniel Winkler.

Another design that Loveless popularized is the full-tapered tang construction in place of the hidden tang method most makers used. (On a hidden-tang knife, a narrow extension of the blade is completely enclosed by the handle made of a stick of wood, antler, or other material. On a full-tang knife, the handle is a full-length exposed extension of the blade sandwiched between handle material slabs. In most cases the metal is tapered to reduce weight and give better balance.) Loveless knives were handier and more functional, and in addition, they exhibited a superior level of workmanship that set the stage for the near perfection achieved by today's makers. Although Loveless is still a very active knifemaker, his knives have achieved almost a cult status with collectors.

Bill Moran of Braddock Heights, Maryland, has been hand-forging knives professionally since 1945. Always considered a top maker, he is a past president of the Knifemakers Guild and one of the founders of the American Bladesmith Society. In 1973 at the Knifemakers Show in Kansas City, Missouri, he pioneered a movement among knifemakers that is now a powerful force—he reintroduced Damascus steel. There are now dozens of Damascus makers in the United States and more on the way. It is perhaps the fastest growing trend in knifemaking. Bill Moran indeed started a revolution. His distinctive handle treatments, utilizing darkly stained curly maple wood with sterling silver inlaid wire in the fashion of the old-time Kentucky rifle builders, is still copied by some makers in "Moran style" knives. Like Loveless, his knives are among the most highly sought-after collectibles ever made.

In the hands of these and other innovative craftsmen, the modern handmade knife has become a paragon of value, function, and artistic expression. But many people, when first introduced to such knives, ask, "Aren't factory knives any good? Are custom knives really any better?"

The answer to both questions is yes. Factory knives are better than ever and are sometimes quite a good value, but a

George Herron kudu horn-handled folder, Raymond Cover sheep horn skinner, and Corbet Sigman stag hunter.

handmade knife from a top maker is distinctly better in materials, workmanship, beauty, and intrinsic value. A good bench-made blade is like a fine custom double-barreled shotgun or a bamboo fly rod: it not only works better than an off-the-shelf specimen but it also gives you a good feeling just to possess and use it.

Custom knives are great collectibles, and those from the best makers tend to appreciate in value. Some purchased five years ago may be worth two or three times as much today. Perhaps the best thing about a truly custom-built knife is that regardless of what a customer wants he will be able to get it from some maker, somewhere.

For example, if a customer fancies a particular type of knife with a handle of exotic tropical hardwood, American hardwood, elephant ivory, fossilized mastodon ivory, wart hog tusk, sambar stag antler, sheephorn, water buffalo horn, pearl, abalone, amber, jade, agate, silver, gold, or a hundred other materials including an everlasting synthetic called Micarta, he can have it. The cost may be $50 or over $15,000, but it can be attained. If a customer needs a good, affordable dropped-point skinner for deer hunting, or if he wants a reproduction of a Persian dagger made entirely of Damascus, or a pearl-handled interframe folder embellished by one of the world's best engravers, he can have those also.

There are two schools of thought prevalent today among knifemakers and collectors concerning the function of a knife— one considers the knife a tool; the other, a work of art. Many makers who began by creating using knives for hunters, fishermen and other outdoorsmen have turned to making display pieces. These "art knives" can sell for several thousand dollars and up— way up. Some of these knives have to be seen to be believed. They most certainly will be museum pieces for future generations.

With such expensive knives on the market, where does that leave the average hunter and fisherman? Not only are there a good number of makers selling highly finished knives for very reasonable prices, but some of the best-known names in the business are now making reasonably priced using knives for the outdoorsman.

I will never forget the first truly fine handmade knife I ever held in my hands. I couldn't believe a knife could be so beautiful. To me it was a sculpture in steel and wood. George Herron, its maker, just watched my naive wonderment over the knife and smiled. "I can't draw too well," he said, puffing on his ever present trademark pipe, "so I just go to work on my grinder and grind away everything that isn't a knife." Herron is a remarkable craftsman who has been called the Grandaddy of South Carolina Knifemakers. Our meeting was nearly twenty years ago and he is still making wonderful knives. "I've always tried to keep my prices reasonable," he says. "I want the average hunter to be able to afford one of my knives."

Herron, of Springfield, South Carolina, has been a full-time maker since 1975 and has made more than five thousand knives. He was one of the first members of the Knifemakers Guild, as well as a past president and director. He is considered by many

A Herron knife in all the stages of the stock removal method of knifemaking.

to be one of the finest makers in the world, as well as one of the most likable. His work is known for impeccable workmanship in knives designed to be used. They are noted for superior design. (He is a longtime deer hunter and owns one rifle with which he has harvested more than one hundred whitetails, so he knows what a using knife ought to be.) He also makes boot and fighting knives and an exquisite folding model. Although quite a few of his blades go to collectors, many are found in use from the swamps of the Palmetto State to the veldts of Africa.

Herron doesn't quote delivery times or prices any more since his backorders approached double digits several years ago (now it's about seven or eight years) but he usually has a few knives for sale at the major knife and sportsman shows. In addition to his regular line, he also makes two satin-finished working models for $75, each complete with a handfitted sheath. "I have always wanted to make an affordable knife for hunters and fishermen," he says. "I can only make about one knife per million people in the U.S. per year. These working knives will allow more people to afford and use my knives."

One respected maker who is creating knives for the collector and user is Corbet Sigman of Liberty, West Virginia. A very personable man who is as likable as they come, his peers have nicknamed him "The Knifemaker's Knifemaker" for his superb craftsmanship. He makes a complete line of beautifully finished outdoor, folding, and survival-type knives for collectors and discriminating users, but also crafts a serviceable working knife for the incredible price of $60, the same sum he put on them a number of years ago. "When I got into knifemaking years ago, I wanted to make a knife people could use. By making working knives I can build a knife for a lot of people. I had gotten away from working knives," Sigman admits. "About 98 percent were going to collectors. The highly finished knives were out of the price range of most users, but by making working knives I can build a knife for a lot of people."

Hunting knives by (from top) George Herron, Dick Hodson, Steve Johnson, and Corbet Sigman.

Another maker who produces finely crafted using knives at extremely reasonable prices is Raymond Cover of Mineral Point, Missouri. His workmanship, with well-executed grind lines and beautiful polish work, is on a par with anyone. His delivery times are short enough so that someone who wants a new hunting knife for next season can get one.

To meet the desires of those who want a folding knife, many makers are crafting finely machined and finished knives that snap open and shut with the precision of a vault. Frank Centofante, of Madisonville, Tennessee, the current president of the Knifemakers Guild, has been crafting folding knives almost exclusively for many years. His magnificent folders come in a number of different styles with handle materials that include pearl and jigged bone.

A maker whose work stopped me at the Guild Show is Ralph Dewey Harris, of Brandon, Florida, who builds a line of interframe folders made of stainless steel or titanium. The stainless models with their inlays of pearl and other exotic materials were lovely. But his titanium folders knocked me out. Flawlessly constructed, they also had gorgeous inlays of pearl and ivory, yet, because of their frame construction, were unbelievably light-weight. The titanium frames were jeweled like a fine rifle bolt and color anodized in gold, bronze, blue/purple, and green. They were striking.

Tommy Lee of Gaffney, South Carolina, has made knives for such sportsmen as John F. Kennedy Jr. and Hank Williams Jr. He has been a prominent knifemaker and big-game hunter for most of his adult life. He began knifemaking as a vocation in 1978 after a number of years of pursuing it as a hobby. A former director of the Knifemakers Guild, his blades have always been recognizable through their simple, classic flowing lines. He uses ATS-34 and 440C stainless steel and Damascus in two patterns.

Jay Hendrickson is an advocate of the forged blade. The Frederick, Maryland, master bladesmith says, "The study of

Fighting knives by (from left) Jimmy Lile, Jim Ence, Jim Hammond, and Harold Corby.

Joe Keeslar's knife is an example of the finest in hand forging.

Jim Weyer

metallurgy shows that high-carbon steel mechanically worked (hammered) above the transformation temperature produces the finest grain possible in steel. It is highly desirable for great strength, toughness and cutting ability in a blade. It is for this reason and a deep personal conviction to produce a superior steel that all blades in my shop are forged." His knives are similar to those produced by the legendary Bill Moran, who lives in the same town, yet have a quality and handsome line of their own. Many feature high-carbon forged blades with curly maple handles that have silver wire inlays similar to the finest Kentucky rifles. Each knife is unique and a work of art.

His philosophy is simple: "There are many of us who are attracted to owning a beautifully designed knife, made by hand, which represents a one-of-a-kind piece that will never be duplicated."

Joe Keeslar of Almo, Kentucky, is a master bladesmith whose magnificent knives reflect his ability to work in several different styles. From massive brass-backed primitive bowies to filed bolster daggers to sterling silver wire-inlaid Mediterranean fighters, they reflect the best in forged blades.

Classic fishing and hunting knives by Herron reflect superb workmanship.

For superlative forged blades in tool steel or Damascus, Don Fogg of Jasper, Alabama, is a highly respected master bladesmith. His art knives are found in some of the finest collections in the world, and he is also making some working models priced for the average outdoorsman. A relocated New Englander, he is also my favorite knifemaking philosopher. "I think it is fair to say this is the age of the bladesmith in American custom knives," he notes. "The forged blade has always been distinguishable from the stock removal blade by its character and style. It was the success of Damascus steel that propelled bladesmithing into the collectible market. It is really quite a remarkable rebirth of the craft."

On the prices of collectible versus using knives Fogg says, "It takes a considerable amount of time to finish a knife well. The finish does not improve the functionality of that knife, but it does add to the cost. When knives are made to be collected, the fit and finish is the most significant aspect, but in a using knife, the extra cost is not easy to justify. More and more makers are returning to making using knives and the knife business is in the process of rediscovering its roots. I see the custom knife business in the United States as an exciting field from both the makers' point of view and from the collectors'. The quality of the craftsmanship has never been higher. The creativity and innovation is exciting."

Fogg is also a partner in Kemal Knives. He is responsible for the Damascus blades while his associate, Murad Sayen of Bryant Pond, Maine, crafts the handles for their knives. Their art knives bring substantial prices and are among the most beautiful cutlery pieces anywhere. Fogg, however, acknowledges that there are some shortcomings to the ancient methods. "Not all Damascus steel is great," he admits. "Some is better than others; we are always experimenting for a superior steel. For an everyday using knife, I'd pick a properly forged blade of high-carbon tool steel. The thing I don't like about stainless is that it stays shiny too long. It looks like something from the fifties. Shiny, as we all know, isn't necessarily good."

Murad Sayen, who designs and makes Kemal handles with an expressiveness that reflects his artistic background, is an accomplished knifemaker who also admires his partner's work. Sayen says of Fogg: "He puts his soul and himself into his blades; he breathes life into them. Magnetism, that's what I say drew us together. It is the synthesis of our partnership. Our knives are pieces of the spirit."

Some of the most popular styles of knives made today are the fighting, boot, and survival models, but probably only a few go to military personnel, cloak-and-dagger types, and urban warfare guerrillas. The sharpened blade is man's oldest weapon and perhaps these lethal implements appeal to our deeply rooted instinct to survive. In some cases they can be so nasty looking that the average person would rather pick up a spider than handle one. Most go to collectors as examples of fine craftsmanship and artistic knifemaking.

For many makers, their first art knife was an interpretation of a historic fighting knife, the legendary bowie. We have been in love with this icon of American history for more than one-hundred-fifty years. For many it has a unique psychological attraction. We want to touch it. We'd like to pick it up and admire its solid weight, but it is almost intimidating. It is a paradox of beauty and terrible function.

To many frontiersmen, Civil War soldiers, and present-day knife collectors, the bowie was and is the ultimate blade. It has the same virtues now it has had for a century and a half. Designed for carving up an attacking adversary, man or beast, into so many harmless pieces, it is physically awesome compared to almost any other knife except a sword. Such an imposing blade of polished steel, from nine to over twelve inches in length, smooth as a maiden's cheek and cold as a hangman's heart, seems to radiate a life of its own.

Picking up a massive razor-sharp bowie is very much like touching a snake. It may not bite you, but there's always that chance. As you run your fingertips lightly down its finely honed edge, there's an involuntary quiver down the back of your spine. You can almost feel it between your ribs, leaking out your life-blood.

Although latently as deadly as any viper, the bowie knife is thought to be the epitome of the very best of the knifemaker's art. Now bowies are being made in many variations such as the

Searles or the Rezin (Spanish) type which is probably the most historically accurate (Rezin Bowie was Jim Bowie's brother and designed the knife he gave to him); there are English bowie reproductions, Confederate bowies, and primitive bowies like those which came from the forging fires of frontier blacksmiths.

Depending on the maker, these modern-day bowie knives can cost from $200 to as much as $3,000 or more. Waiting periods for these creations can be from only a few months to about the time your kid will finish college, if he or she's in kindergarten now.

If your taste leans to big knives, especially for historically correct bowies, Alex Daniels of Town Creek, Alabama, is crafting some extraordinary examples. I saw Daniels's work this past summer at the Guild show in Orlando and his knives stopped me in my tracks. You will not find better workmanship and eye for line. And I've seen comparable knives made by some famous makers selling for several times his prices. He also makes a complete line of hunting models.

To understand the status of the bowie in our history, we must examine the misty stories surrounding it since its birth in the early 1800s. Much of the bowie's past is shrouded in hearsay and myth, but whether true or not, it was a wonderfully romantic start to a legend.

As the story goes, a certain wealthy Louisiana land speculator named Jim Bowie was having a nasty feud with a fellow named Major Norris Wright. Around 1825 they got into an argument in the street of a Southern frontier town. Wright became so angry that he pulled a gun and shot at Bowie. Whether he hit him or not is uncertain, but if hit, Bowie was relatively unhurt. In a rage, Bowie also pulled a gun but couldn't get it to go off.

Then they resorted to fisticuffs until onlookers finally separated the two men. Soon after this ugly affair, Jim's brother Rezin gave him his personal knife for protection. It was straight pointed with a blade slightly over nine inches long and one-and-

Massive frontier-style bowie with stag handle by Lile.

a-half inches wide. Rezin evidently figured, like many frontiers-men came to believe, that you didn't have to worry if a knife would fire or not in the heat of a fracas.

However, this knife was not the bowie that later gained so much fame. Although Rezin's knife had served him well, Jim had other ideas about what made the ideal fighting blade. Some-time around 1830, it is said, Jim Bowie visited a well-known blacksmith named James Black in Washington, Arkansas. Black claimed to have a secret process for tempering steel, which he later took to his grave. Bowie gave the craftsman a wooden model of a blade that he wanted. When Bowie returned, Black had made two knives, one like Bowie had ordered and another of his own design. Bowie liked the blacksmith's knife the best, and thus the legendary bowie knife was born.

Only six years after he obtained the knife from James Black, Jim Bowie and the knife that carries his name met their ultimate fate. After twelve days of siege, on March 6, 1836, Jim Bowie, Davy Crockett, Colonel William Travis, and more than one-hun-dred-fifty brave men died at the Alamo fighting for Texas inde-pendence from Mexico. What happened to the original bowie knife is not known. Some think it was carried off by a Mexican soldier, others say it was burned with Bowie at the Alamo. What-ever happened to it, it helped shape the American frontier.

From 1830 on, as the legend of the bowie grew, suddenly everyone had to have one. Mountain men carried them West; Indians feared the "longknives" who used them with terrible ef-ficiency. In the South and West many men felt undressed with-out one. Congressmen wore them in Washington. The bowie craze lasted throughout the Civil War, when many soldiers relied on their knives in close combat. Confederate troops, especially, utilized bowies and even had their own version, known as the Arkansas Toothpick (double edged all the way down the blade.)

After the Civil War the bowie's popularity waned, but it has influenced American knifemaking to this day. Most of us, if over thirty years old, had for our first real hunting knife a smaller version of a bowie with a five- or six-inch clip-pointed blade. Only in the past fifteen to twenty years has the drop-pointed hunting knife become so popular.

The bowie knife has achieved a place in America's history that few other weapons can match. Along with such important destiny shapers as the Kentucky rifle and Colt .45 six-shooter, the bowie knife is an important part of our heritage.

In addition to the bowie knives, makers are re-creating every kind of exalted blade from the pages of history. Walk down the aisles of the Knifemakers Guild Show and you may see re-creations of the opulent blades of the San Francisco gold rush days, Japanese ceremonial tantos, Roman swords, Persian daggers, the stocking knives of Scottish clansmen, and every type of dagger, scimitar and dirk imaginable. In the past there were even a few makers crafting gentlemen's knife-and-fork sets reminiscent of those bygone days when a weary traveler needed his own eating utensils to maintain his dignity at some remote way station.

Many knifemakers have their best work enhanced by world-class engravers and scrimshanders to create display pieces. If done well, this can add greatly to the value of the finished knife. Several other makers are doing all of their own work including engraving and scrimshaw. The market for high-art knives seems to be strong even though there are a limited number of patrons who can afford them.

A young knifemaker who I believe is one of the rising superstars is Daniel Winkler of Blowing Rock, North Carolina. With his longish hair and a full beard, you might think he just stepped out of the French and Indian Wars. Actually that is where his personal convictions lie. He was the knifemaker who crafted the knives and tomahawks for the principal actors in the motion picture *The Last of the Mohicans*. Winkler is a member of The Guild, American Blacksmith Society, The American Mountain

Men, and various reenactment groups. He forges folders, belt and hunting knives, period reproductions such as riflemen's knives, and other custom designs. His work is admired by several makers who build entirely different knives, yet recognize Winkler's talents. Winkler's business associate, Karen Shook, helps with administrative duties and makes beautiful period-authentic sheaths for the knives. Each is a museum piece in its own right.

Another name that came to the forefront in custom knifemaking by way of the big screen was that of the late Jimmy Lile, "The Arkansas Knifesmith." He made the big lethal-looking fighting knives for the movies *Rambo* and *First Blood*, which started a whole new trend in fighting and survival knives that continues today. A knifemaker since 1970, Lile passed away a couple of years ago, but his family continues making fine custom knives in Russellville, Arkansas.

Regardless of what you may desire in a custom knife, whether it is a hunting model, big scary looking fighter, bank vault opening and closing folder, or some exotic dream knife that has been roaming your subconscious, there are fine craftsmen in shops across the country who will build a blade for you that is a pleasure to use and a treasure to own.

CLASSIC & PRECISION RIFLES

Jere Eggleston rifle combines fine stock and metalwork with beautiful walnut.

CLASSIC &
PRECISION
RIFLES

Deep smoky hues of chestnut and chocolate ripple across earthy gold in the walnut's hand-rubbed finish. Lustrous blue-black metalwork accents the wood's beauty, appearing as if it grew there. Exacting crisscrossing lines, hand cut precisely into the stock at 24 lines to the inch, create a flowing pattern on the graceful curves of the wood.

These attributes describe a highly evolved American art form, the custom-made classic-stocked hunting rifle, a statement of subdued elegance and efficiency—one of the finest firearms in history. These masterpieces are made by craftsmen, individually or at times in collaboration with others, working in basements, garages, and modern workshops across the nation.

Some are relatively simple and utilitarian: although they exhibit beautiful workmanship, they are intended to be used, to be carried into the field. Others are virtual museum pieces of incredible craftsmanship, world-class engraving, magnificent rare wood, and skillful metalsmithing. The rifles of no other country or of no other era approach their excellence of line or craftsmanship. They are simply unchallenged.

Wouldn't it be wonderful someday to own the very finest of a particular item that had ever been produced? Especially if that item is a handsome rifle made to your order. It would be a dream come true. Can't happen, you say. Like some of the bespoken shotguns created in England or Italy, such a gun costs as much as a house on the lake complete with a sailboat. Besides, even if you were a baron or duke, and could afford such a prize, it would take four or five years to get one.

Well, although not exactly inexpensive, some custom rifles can be made affordable for many sportsmen. There are makers who build what would be called a semicustom rifle, taking a factory barreled action, adding a custom floorplate/trigger bow assembly, and then stocking it with a nice piece of walnut. All of this can be accomplished for something less than a king's ransom. On the other side, there are full-blown, exhibition-quality

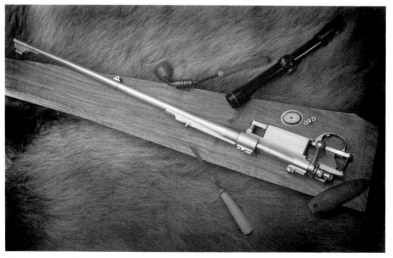

A custom metalsmithing job in the white before stocking begins.

custom guns with a great deal of metalsmithing and engraving that are extremely pricey. But they are not usually intended to be bumped and bruised in the field anyway. Best of all, some makers will take an order for a rifle after hunting season and can deliver your new gun by next year. Or maybe the next season.

Of course, this type of rifle may not be for everybody. "Classic" refers to the style of stock exhibited in most custom rifles built these days. The lines on a classic stock are all portions of a circle. Nothing is sharp or angular. If you prefer the so-called California-style stock then you are probably out of luck. At least 99 percent of all the custom-made rifles produced in the United States today are built in the classic mold.

California-style rifles have certainly taken game all over the world, but they have a few intrinsic flaws. When a rifle is referred to as California style it generally means the type of stock, but the rest of the gun is important as well. Such stocks usually have a shiny epoxy finish. Their slanted fore-end and flared grip cap of contrasting wood may be set off by white spacers, and the rest of the package includes a high Monte Carlo comb with large cheekpiece, skipline check-

Eggleston custom rifle built with a fine piece of California English walnut.

ering or oak leaf carving, and a squared boxy fore-end. Some of the most radical examples have rollover cheekpieces that look like a surfer's dream wave.

With all of this goes a high-polish bluing on the barrel and receiver. Unfortunately for the sportsman who might actually want to hunt with such a flashy gun, shiny finishes on wood and metal are just great for letting a deer or elk know your exact location. Overstated Monte Carlo buttstocks are an excellent way to ensure maximum recoil. Sadly, the biggest flaw for many is simply a matter of taste. Discriminating sportsmen just don't go for that gloss and overstated flashy pretense.

The classic style hunting rifle generally has a time-consuming, hand-rubbed oil finish that is in the wood, not on it, or a subdued synthetic finish that lets the beauty of the wood show through. The buttstock has a high, thick comb that is straight. If there is a cheekpiece, it is a gracefully sculpted continuation of the stock's lines, and the fore-end has a comfortable rounded configuration. Checkering can run as fine as 28 lines-per-inch in wraparound fleur-de-lis or multipoint patterns. The contrasting fore-end tip, if there is one, may be of horn or ebony, and all blued surfaces have a low-luster finish. Overall the work must blend the rifle into a refined and practical gun that won't spook game, and exhibits an excellence that only superior hand-craftsmanship can provide.

When you commission a riflemaker or stockmaker to build a gun for you, the finished product will be individually yours. Like the double-barreled game guns of England, you can choose the final appearance of the rifle so long as you stay within the parameters of your stockmaker's style. It will be your choices of action, wood, checkering, engraving, fore-end treatment, butt plate or pad, grip cap, barrel length and contour, sights, comb treatment, and caliber that makes the gun custom built just for you. The rifle can be made superlight for mountain use or beefed up for one of the mighty magnum calibers, perhaps for heavy game in Africa. It may be completely the work of a single craftsman or of several artisans. A stockmaker, metalsmith, bluing expert, and engraver may all contribute to the finished piece. However it is accomplished, you will possess a rifle that is uniquely yours and not a copy of anything else.

All of this sounds great, so how do you get started? After choosing your riflemaker, you must procure an action on which to base the rifle. By far the most popular actions are the pre-1964 Winchester Model 70, various incarnations of the Model 98 military Mausers, and the Ruger No. 1. The first two are bolt actions and the third is a falling block single shot. Price for a pre-'64 Model 70 will start at about $500 and go up depending on caliber and condition. A good Mauser action will begin at a couple of hundred bucks or so but it must then be extensively reworked by a metalsmith at a cost at least $1,000 to $2,000. The price for a complete rebuild can go over $5,000. Ruger No. 1 actions can be bought from about $300 to $400.

The second largest, and most visible expense (and in many cases the most costly) is the wood from which the stock will be carved. Most cus-

Inletting an action requires many hours of cutting and fitting to assure a precise fit.

Checkering the gun stock can take more than 50 percent of the time required to make a custom stock.

tom rifles will have some type of walnut as stock wood. A few stocks may be made of maple, cherry, or myrtlewood, but they represent a tiny percentage.

Of the walnuts, the most desired is what used to be called French walnut (*Juglans regia*) because France is where much of it came from, though little originates from there now. A genuine high-quality French walnut blank is rare indeed. Most stockmakers generically call this wood Circassian or English walnut today. Labeled the "royal walnut," it goes by many other names, like Turkish, New Zealand, or Spanish because it is harvested in those locales. It is all basically the same wood. Many stockers are now using English walnut from California, a strikingly beautiful wood that characteristically has dark brown or black streaks running through a much lighter brown or even blonde background. Blanks can range from $250 to more than $2,000. Presentation marble-cake configurations (a cloudy, smoky grain pattern with swirling deep brown accents) bring the premium prices. Good English walnut has excellent properties, being very hard and dense yet fairly light. It has tiny pores and takes precise inletting and checkering better than any other gunstock wood. It has been said that it has the hardness and consistency of elephant ivory and yet carves like imported cheese.

Other choices are black walnut, Claro, and Bastogne. They have many good attributes but are not as popular as Circassian or English with stockmakers or discriminating customers.

Black walnut (*Juglans nigra*) is the least expensive, with a good blank priced at about half that of an English blank. It is a good stock wood and is the walnut of choice on most factory guns. A little heavier than English, it takes checkering fairly well and is available in a broad array of grain and color variations. It is seen at its best in the feathercrotch "flame" grain stocks used on vintage high-grade Winchester Model 21 doubles.

Claro (*Juglans hindsii*) is popular with sportsmen who want a showy piece of wood at reasonable cost. It is utilized on many of the more expensive factory rifles, but it is the softest of the walnuts and will not take fine checkering as well as the other species.

Bastogne, or as it has been called, Paradox walnut, is a hybrid of English and Claro and has some of the properties of each. Though a little heavy, it is very strong and is an excellent choice for heavy-caliber rifles. Because it is a hybrid, it can cost almost as much as the better English blanks.

After action and wood blank are chosen and the customer is measured, the stockmaker can begin work. Here is an example of how a riflemaker might take the gun from raw materials to its final form. (He might do all of the work himself or have some of it done by other craftsmen.)

- Stockmaker lays out profile of the stock on the blank.
- Metalsmithing is done to action, and custom sights are fabricated, if desired. (This is usually done by a separate craftsman and may take from several months to a couple of years to complete.)
- Action is sent off to have a premium barrel fitted.
- Inletting is started.
- Stockmaker machines or hand-works blank (the above steps take thirty to fifty hours on average).
- Final sanding of wood in preparation for stock finish.
- Stock finish is applied. (If oil is used, this can take up to twenty-five coats and over a month.)
- Checkering begins (thirty to fifty hours average).
- Gun is sent off to be engraved (months to years).
- Barreled action is blued (usually by someone other than the stockmaker).
- Action is received by stockmaker and put into the finished stock.
- Scope is fitted.
- Rifle is sighted in for accuracy and shipped to customer.

This all happens smoothly only if everything goes well for the riflemaker. Obviously a good deal of shipping time is involved. It is easy to see why it takes six months to several years to get a finished gun. But then it has all been done expressly for you, and when that lovely expression of the gunmaker's art arrives at your doorstep, it is worth the wait.

To promote the business of crafting such guns, the American Custom Gunmakers Guild was formed in 1983. It has in its ranks gunmakers from across the United States. Each year since its inception the Guild has sponsored a rifle to be raffled off. It is a collaborative project, usually worked on by a stockmaker, metalsmith, engraver and a case maker. Not only has a custom action been used but also Mausers, an Enfield, a Springfield, a Ruger No. 1, and an L.C. Smith shotgun action, in addition to a completely custom flintlock.

Some of the work being done by custom gunmakers today has to be seen to be believed. One such maker is D'Arcy Echols of Providence, Utah. His specialty is classic, straight comb sporters. A full-time maker since 1978, he apprenticed with well-known riflemaker Jerry Fisher. Because of his attention to detail, Echols completes only four rifles a year. Now a year and a half behind in orders, his rifles reside in the upper echelon of custom guns. His basic charge is $5,000 for the labor, with the customer supplying the action, stock blank, and barrel ($1,500 to $3,000 depending on the parts). If a full-blown metalsmithing job is to be done, the tariff by the gunmaker is another $5,000 to $7,000 depending on accessories. That is before any engraving is added to the equation. Sound a bit pricey? Well it is, but not when compared to other bespoken guns like an English best, for example, which will cost from three to four times as much and will take from four to five years to acquire. Even a relatively plain English magazine rifle will cost more. With an Echols rifle you get what you pay for—superb workmanship and knowledge of what makes a great rifle.

D'Arcy Echols custom classic-stocked rifle.

Ryne Hazer

Let's take a close look at what is required just to do the metalwork on an Echols rifle (not counting the countless hours involved in the stock) built on a pre-'64 Winchester Model 70 action in .300 Winchester Magnum caliber (a Mauser action would take additional work):

1. Precision grind and detail action:
   A. Re-establish all flats, contours, and radii (clean them up for symmetry since the action was built in a factory).
   B. Fabricate (that means make) and install four-shot magnum magazine and follower. Alter and polish feed rails and feed ramp.
   C. Fabricate checkered bolt stop.
   D. Fabricate right-hand slant trigger assembly. Precision finish and set trigger let off for appropriate poundage.
   E. Precision finish interior dimensions of action for operational smoothness.

Okay, so the action has been worked on, now come the barrel and other parts.

2. Install air gauge (high quality and precise) chrome moly barrel. Chamber for cartridge.
3. Fabricate (it's that word again) custom floorplate, trigger bow, and magazine assembly.
4. Fabricate and install scope mount system (custom designed by Echols).
5. Fabricate new bolt knob and checker the bolt knob with rosette-bordered pattern.
6. Engrave lettering of caliber, company name, and serial number. Other light engraving.
7. All appropriate metal is polished and rust blued. Bolt body and follower damascene finished.

You can easily see that there is a tremendous amount of work that goes into a true custom rifle.

Echols calls his guns "functional elegance that endures." Not only are they beautiful, but they work well. A big-game guide during the elk and mule deer season, he has also been to Africa, not only to hunt but to experience the shooting and functional problems that occur in that most demanding and unforgiving of gamefields—"to address my clients' needs," as he puts it. As a matter of fact, he wants his customers to use their rifles and hunt hard with them. He knows they expect a good-shooting gun as well as a good-looking one.

When asked about the current interest in custom-made synthetic stocked rifles that, while they are not as beautiful as his creations, are, in some cases (like those made by accuracy guru Kenny Jarrett), incredibly accurate, Echols gives a surprising answer. "Rifles built by Kenny Jarrett are not a threat to me. In fact, he has served an important function in custom gunmaking. He has punched the envelope, so to speak. He has made me get better. More emphasis on the sub-minute of angle rifle makes us as custom makers get more accurate."

"I know that a one-minute of angle rifle (minute of angle is one inch at 100 yards, two inches at 200 yards; that is, three shots into one inch at 100 yards) is one to cherish, but I also know that I would look like an idiot to charge what I do for a rifle that shoots an inch and a half," he says. "When you think of the price of a safari and what it costs to secure the trophies a client has dreamed about, the damn thing had better shoot and function right or my name is mud."

Each one of his rifles is tested and retested for reliability and then shot at least one hundred times to check for accuracy and the proper factory load. His rifles shoot exceptionally well. One way he can ensure that is to use a pantograph machine to hog off most of the excess wood from the stock before he starts the precision inletting process. It just saves unproductive time. "The bottom line is the finished product," he says with conviction. "By using the machine to take off the excess wood it allows me to make a living and spend more time on detail work and downrange performance. I want my rifles to be functional as well as elegant."

Most of his clients end up buying at least two rifles, one for light game and a heavier, bigger-bore for tough game like that found in Africa or for the big North American bears. "There is no such thing as an all-around rifle," the gunmaker insists. "It doesn't exist." For a lot of his customers buying an

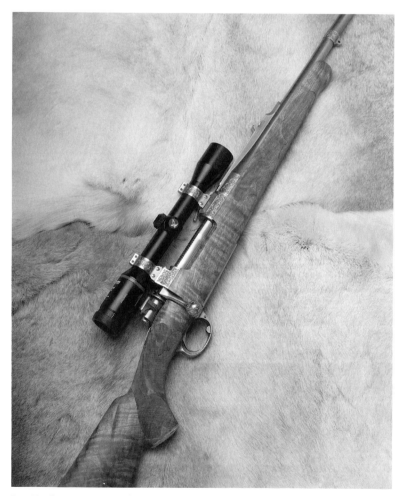

Jere Eggleston custom rifle.

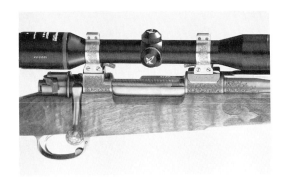

Detail of a fully-engraved custom rifle by Jere Eggleston. All appropriate metalwork is engraved, including action, scope rings, barrel, sights, grip cap, bolt knob, and floorplate.

Echols rifle is like eating a potato chip; it is hard to stop with just one.

Jere Eggleston is a transplanted New Englander who has built fine classic rifles in Columbia, South Carolina, for nearly eighteen years. A master cabinetmaker who has crafted some phenomenal re-creations of period furniture for his family, he has been making rifle stocks since the age of fourteen, when he restocked a favorite .22. An avid big-game hunter, he has taken a dozen species of North American big game including Dall and Stone sheep and Alaskan brown bear. Along with those trophies he has taken two Scottish red stags and loves to duck hunt and chase South Carolina whitetails. A past vice president of the Gunmaker's Guild, he works on only one gun at a time, carrying it through more than eighty hours of hand work as he does everything without the use of machines.

Eggleston has very definite ideas on what constitutes a good rifle stock. For example, his stocks do not have a cheekpiece or fore-end tip. He feels his high, thick comb does the job just as well as a cheekpiece. "A cheekpiece is pure ornamentation, a redundancy that can be left off," he says with assurance. "It doesn't make for a trim stock."

Instead of a fore-end tip Eggleston fashions a handsome schnabel. His love for schnabels goes back to his boyhood years when he admired an uncle's fine German hunting rifles.

"I'll admit that my schnabel may be considered a flourish by some," he admits, "but to me it is a classic, graceful method of terminating the awkward end of a stock."

A special feature of Eggleston's early stocks was a comfortably shaped grip that had a slight palm swell but was very trim, with a skeleton grip cap he carved from $\frac{3}{16}$-inch steel. He now makes his grips even trimmer to comply with the fashion of today's rifles. (I have an Eggleston rifle with the old style grip and happen to think it is the most comfortable I have ever felt on any rifle.)

An example of an elegantly styled Sharon Farmer-Dressel rifle.

The gunmaker uses reworked Mauser or pre-'64 Winchester Model 70 actions as the basis of his guns. And, although he will use a steel butt plate if the customer wants it, he prefers a good rubber pad for working rifles (leather covered in the tradition of the English shotgun makers). Steel butt plates are prone to slip. Showing his big-game hunting experience, he asks, "who wants a rifle that won't stand up in the corner of a hunting cabin?"

Most of his production was originally for sportsmen who intended to use his guns in the field, but in recent years many have been created for those who want the finest in wood, metalsmithing, engraving, and custom-cased accessories—a complete exhibition-quality custom rifle. These rifles may never see the woods, but they are admired as examples of the best in custom classic rifle building. He currently charges $2,500 for the stocking labor on one of his guns, with materials, metalsmithing, and other extras adding to the price. I think they are real bargains in the custom rifle arena.

Paul Dressel, Jr. and Sharon Farmer-Dressel are custom riflemakers in Yakima, Washington. They build bolt-action and single-shot rifles and stock shotguns as well. Paul, who is self-

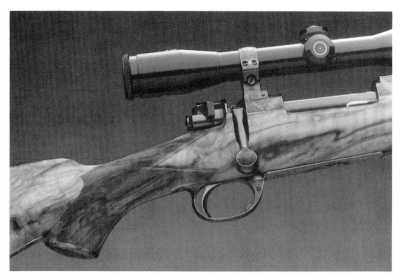

Paul Dressel, Jr.'s custom rifles are a study in simple beauty and function.

taught, and Sharon, who went to gunsmithing school, are a unique team in that as husband and wife they both build guns on their own and also work together on some projects. They are busy folks. Paul still runs his family's roofing business, and he and Sharon also import high-grade Turkish walnut and sell grip caps of their design to the trade. "I wouldn't know what to do if I only had to work forty hours a week," he says. "I work that much a lot of times in three days."

He has been in the gunmaking business for thirty-five years and Sharon has been full time since 1982. They prefer to work on full custom projects, with their labor costing about $4,500 on average, and the completed project usually running $25,000 to $30,000. Current delivery is two years. As Paul puts it, he is looking for interesting guns to work on. "I'm as independent as a hog on ice. I just want my next gun to be better than the last."

Mike Gervais is an young gunmaker in Salt Lake City, Utah. A full-time builder for the past three years, he likes to work on any gun as long as it is in good taste. Although his work is excellent and he gets $2,500 for a stock, he admits that he is self

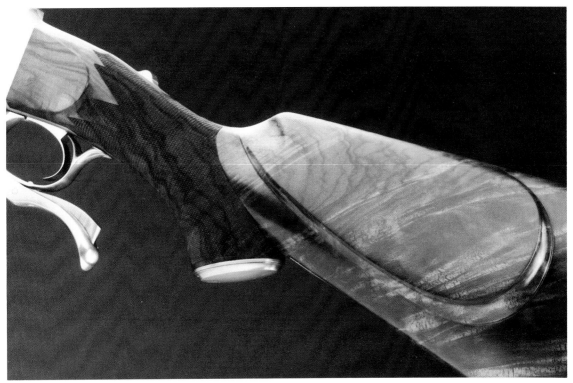

Paul Dressel's Ruger No. 1 with a gracefully sculpted cheekpiece.

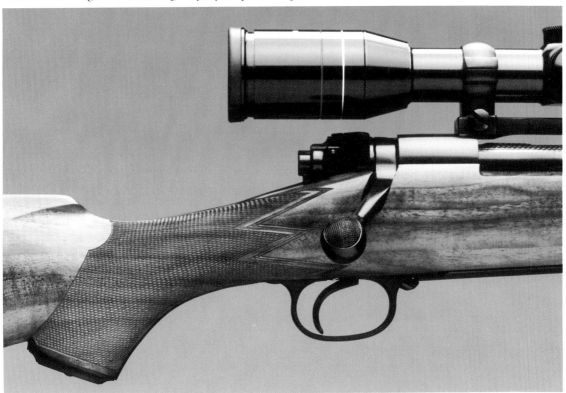

The essence of a Sharon Farmer-Dressel custom rifle is beautifully executed checkering.

taught. "I learned the hard way," he laughs, "but I just like to be carving on a piece of good wood." A cabinetmaker by trade, his ability with his medium and his appreciation for fine woodwork has helped. "I build classically styled rifles that stretch the confines of the neo-American classic rifle," he says. Although synthetic stocks don't bother him, and indeed he hunts with one occasionally, he feels the rifle stocked with fine walnut is important. "I think it is part of the American hunting experience. It is bound in tradition."

Some of the kinds of guns he likes to work on are, as he terms it, "serious guns for silly shooting." In other words, for plinking. He has a personal bolt-action .22 rimfire he made that has tin cans engraved on the butt plate. A marvelous craftsman, he also has a sense of humor.

And now, I am going to do you a favor. A big favor. I'm going to tell you who makes the world's most accurate hunting rifle. That's right. You may notice I didn't say *one* of the most accurate, but *the* most accurate. That's a pretty bold statement, but I think it's true and so do a number of the nation's top firearms experts.

To get one of these phenomenal rifles, you must contact a red-bearded, tobacco-chewing good-ol'-boy who lives down a secondary road outside of Jackson, South Carolina. He wears suspenders every day because of one too many plates of pork chops and grits, and his Southern drawl is laced with entertaining colloquialisms.

His name is Kenny Jarrett, and he is the guru of accuracy—the baron of the beanfield rifle.

If you're a hunter from the South, you already know what a beanfield rifle is, but for the rest of you, it's an ultra-deadly rifle/cartridge combination for taking white-tailed deer on large fields of soybeans or other crops. Shots typically approach 300 to 400 yards. Hunting big clearcuts demands the same type of rifle, one that fires a cartridge having high velocity and pinpoint accuracy.

Just how good are Jarrett's rifles? Though he doesn't guarantee any set standard of accuracy, no rifle leaves his shop until it delivers a three-shot group of .50-inch at 100 yards in .25 caliber or smaller. For larger calibers he expects at most .75 inch. Most of his rifles do better. Some do a lot better. I know several Jarrett owners whose rifles will shoot into a quarter-inch circle all day long. The best three-shot grouping with my own .300 Winchester Magnum has been .354 inch, and it will cluster jagged, one-hole groups about .400-inch day in and day out.

Sounds incredible, but it's true. Just ask the bear guide I had in Alberta a few years ago. After my long flight to Canada, he asked me to check my rifle by shooting at a target stuck into a sandbar 100 yards away. His jaw nearly fell into the sand when I shot several half-inch groups. He was used to seeing clients' rifles shoot $1\frac{1}{2}$ to $2\frac{1}{2}$ inches or more, not a half-minute of angle.

On a recent elk-hunting trip, upon arrival in camp, I went to the shooting range with my guide to check out my rifle. I had told him beforehand how well my Jarrett shot, but he

Kenny Jarrett using a sophisticated optic microscope to check the rifling in one of his new hand-lapped barrels.

only smiled a typical guide's "I've heard that one before" smile. I could understand why he was so skeptical. In the back of his truck were a number of targets shot by the other clients before I arrived. The groups ranged from a couple of inches at best to all over the target. I settled down at the bench and fired three careful shots at a hundred yards. While I waited he went to retrieve the target, and as he made his way back to the shooting bench I could see amazement on his face. I had already seen through the scope how good the group was. "This is the best group any of my clients has ever shot," he said, obviously pleased as he held up the target with all three bullets clustered into the same hole. That is what I have come to expect from Jarrett rifles. Four days later, a 175-yard shot collected a mature 6X6 bull elk.

Rifles like Jarrett's have universal appeal. They are ideal for almost every type of long-range shooting situation, like cross-canyon shots at elk or mule deer, or that once-in-a-lifetime try for a trophy bighorn. For Africa's dangerous game, where shot placement is critical, a Jarrett rifle is a good insurance policy.

Do you really need this kind of rifle, especially if all you do is hunt whitetails in thick cover where you might not be able to see past 50 yards? Maybe not, but wouldn't it be great to place your bullet perfectly when only a small portion of the vital area is exposed? That's what makes a Jarrett rifle such a confidence builder. You *know* where the bullet is going to hit. Confidence in your rifle breeds success in the field.

Kenny Jarrett, now in his early forties, was a soybean farmer on his uncle's ten-thousand-acre Cowden Plantation until 1979, when he turned to gunsmithing full time. He became interested in bench-rest shooting, and before long won a number of competitions. It became a passion. Kenny personally holds six world records, and his rifles have established nine more.

Since his first love was hunting, Jarrett began applying his gunsmithing techniques toward the development of super-

Jarrett rifles are capable of incredible accuracy the first time, every time.

accurate hunting rifles, which now account for most of his yearly one hundred-gun production.

"I'm a hopeless, helpless fanatic when it come to making a gun right," says Kenny. "It's just something personal with me to try for perfection. You hear some people say 'well it's good enough to be a deer rifle.' Well, 'good enough' isn't in my vocabulary. I want to make that son-of-a-bitch as perfect as if I were going to pack it up and take it to a world championship shoot."

Kenny's field exploits back up his obsession with accuracy. Two of his most memorable shots include a gemsbok taken in Africa at 557 yards, and a groundhog measured at 700 yards. His field laboratory has yielded over 150 deer at distances from 300 to 500 yards.

My most spectacular shot with a Jarrett rifle was a prairie dog killed at a stepped-off 512 yards. On the same excursion, I also shot sixteen dogs out of one box of 20 cartridges, all at over 300 yards. In both instances I was using factory ammunition! Proud of these achievements, when I boasted of them to Kenny he just smiled and said, "Too bad you weren't using some of our handloads to really see what that rifle can do. Before you left on that trip my 16-year-old son shot a .095-inch group with that rifle at one hundred yards!"

Each Jarrett rifle incorporates a little hocus-pocus, along with know-how and hard work. Kenny and his staff of gunsmiths work in what has to be one of the most modern and precision-oriented gunshops anywhere.

Says Jarrett, "Our rifles come from hand crafting, innovation, and constant attention to quality. My customers deserve the best, and we don't just do it right for some people—we do it for everybody." Then grinning, he adds, "When you get one of my rifles, your other rifles will gather dust because you won't want to shoot them any more."

If you suspect a lot of this is unfounded praise, consider what these shooting experts think of Jarrett's work:

Dave Petzal, executive editor and co-shooting editor of *Field & Stream*: "I own five Jarrett rifles and have shot probably six times that many. They are capable of impossible accuracy not in the realm of discussion ten years ago. Jarrett rifles are absolutely the most accurate in the world."

Layne Simpson, field editor for *Shooting Times*: "I've shot many rifles and Jarrett's are the most accurate big-game rifles I've shot—by far."

Another adherent is Jim Carmichael, shooting editor of *Outdoor Life*: "Kenny Jarrett has explored exciting new territory in the development of the long-range hunting rifle. He has led the way in truly effective long-range hunting rifles and cartridges. His blend of cartridge performance know-how and rifle-building skills have made him a leader in state-of-the-art accuracy. With a Jarrett rifle, long-range hunting is not a theory, but a reality."

Most Jarrett rifles begin as a Remington 700 action (Kenny's favorite), though he occasionally uses a custom action. Next, he fits a match-made grade, bench-rest quality stainless steel barrel meticulously crafted right there in his own shop. The stock will be a McMillan fiberglass—no other need apply. Many other options are available, such as stock and metal finish.

One option I like is Kenny's design for a muzzle brake to reduce recoil. My .300 Magnum, for example, kicks about like a .243. On the big boys, it can really save your shoulder and reduce flinching. That means more accuracy. He will also break in the barrel by shooting it and carefully cleaning between groups, and then develop the best load for that particular rifle. Most rifles are delivered with a box of handloads tuned to the gun.

A new addition to the Jarrett lineup is a sweet little number he calls the "Walkabout." Built on the Remington Model 7 action with a twenty- or twenty-one-inch medium-weight barrel, it weighs in at just under seven pounds with scope. A better, handier rifle for packing up a mountainside or for treestand use cannot be imagined. And, it will shoot a half-minute of angle.

Jarrett rifles may not seem beautiful. There is no burled walnut and no soft rust bluing. But there's an old saying: "Beauty is only skin deep, but ugly goes to the bone." An inaccurate hunting rifle is ugly, so when you really think about it, that makes Jarrett's rifles downright beautiful because they perform better than any other.

Each Jarrett gun incorporates superb craftsmanship and attention to even the most minute details. He machines two metal pillars to fit the receiver, then epoxies them into the stock. Thus, when the receiver screws are tightened, the metal-to-metal fit is precise and stress free. The action and barrel are trued and squared to each other, and he works the bolt way and the bolt face until they are perfectly parallel to the barrel threads. In fact, the barreled action can be removed from the stock and replaced without changing zero. Kenny also massages the trigger to create a light, creep-free pull that breaks like fine crystal.

If everything goes together okay, but the rifle still doesn't shoot right, Kenny will take it apart and painstakingly re-check everything. Back when he used other companies' barrels he sometimes changed them two or three times. Once, he became so frustrated with a particular rifle that he cut it in two! (Surprising what a high-speed band saw can do to a finished gun.) The pieces now hang on the wall in his shop, testimony to visitors that "good enough" does not exist in Kenny's world.

For checking his new rifles, Jarrett has a 100-, 200- and even a 600-yard range, and is currently building a testing facility that will stretch an amazing 1,000 yards. He doesn't guess what his guns and cartridges will do at these distances—he knows.

Jarrett builds many guns for wildcat cartridges, including several he has designed. Currently his most popular cartridge is his own 300 Jarrett, which is based on an 8mm Magnum case that has been necked down with a new shoulder. Accuracy and power are phenomenal. You can be sure cartridge development at Jarrett is ongoing.

He is also producing several hunting handguns, including one on a Remington XP100 action that will shoot at least as accurately as his rifles. I own a Ruger Super Redhawk, which Kenny customized into his Ultimate Redhawk. My first three-shot group at 50 yards with full-blown .300 grain .44 Magnum hunting loads went $^5/_8$-inch—incredible for a revolver. With judicious load development, it will shoot all six shots into a three- to four-inch group at 100 yards.

Jarrett with the infamous rifle that he cut in two because it would not perform to his expectations.

The basic price of a Jarrett rifle is about $3,000; extensive options may hike the cost to as much as $4,500. That may seem expensive, but consider this: how expensive is missing a shot at the biggest trophy you've ever seen?

"If your rifle ain't accurate," drawls Jarrett, "you might as well have a pocketful of firecrackers, 'cause all you'll have is a noisemaker.

"But hell, there's no magic in what I do. It ties directly to education, trial-and-error, and beating my head against the wall until it's right."

And then, settling back into his chair with a cold beer in one grimy fist, he smiles, "I never wanted to be rich...I just wanted to be the best."

MUZZLELOADERS

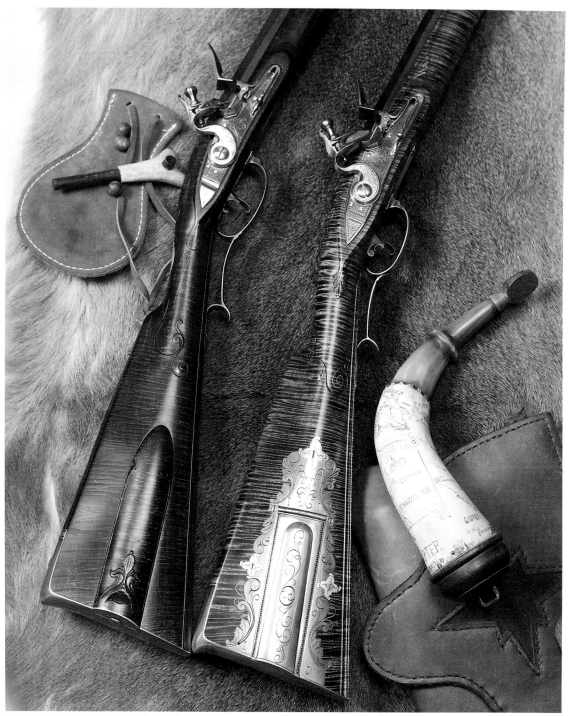

Custom flintlock muzzleloading rifles by Mike Gahagan (left) and Jim Chambers.

MUZZLELOADERS

A great cloud of white smoke hangs heavy in the morning air and the acrid smell of burned blackpowder fills the woods with its familiar and somehow reassuring odor. The boom of the rifle reverberates off the surrounding forest and echoes in the hills and valleys beyond. Downrange a sphere of pure lead finds its mark.

It is a scene which has been reenacted countless times since our forefathers first landed on these shores more than three hundred years ago. The lure of the blackpowder muzzleloading rifle or fowling piece is as strong for many today as it was for Daniel Boone, Davy Crockett, Kit Carson, and all of the other pioneers who explored and shaped our land.

They feel a sense of heritage when they shoot, hunt with, or simply admire a fine reproduction of a firearm that made history and shaped our destiny in the eighteenth and nineteenth centuries. Some have taken their love of the old blackpowder burners to its ultimate height, the building of beautiful and functional muzzleloaders.

With no other kind of firearm does the owner have such a sense of "the way things used to be" as with muzzleloading rifles and smoothbores. Their rich history goes back to the initial days spent on these shores by the colonists.

The earliest guns to reach this land were muskets from the Dutch, and single- and double-barreled rifles and fowlers from England and France. They were slim and long of barrel. Homesteaders used them to provide meat for their families just as they had done in their motherland. Many settlers in Pennsylvania were of Germanic birth and they brought with them short, heavy barreled, large caliber flintlock rifles that were called Jaegers. Used for hunting (the word *jaeger* means hunter), they were highly developed guns with intricate carvings and other embellishments to show the artistic pride of the gunsmith in his work. The Hudson Bay area found many French smoothbores in use; called *Fusil De Chasse* (guns for hunting), they had very long barrels and could be used for shot or ball. Later Northwest Guns became popular for the same reasons and remained so for many years in the region.

Then, starting before the Revolution and for the next quarter of a century, a type of firearm began to take shape that would become one of the most highly evolved and celebrated guns in our history. Called the Pennsylvania rifle (after 1800 it became known as the Kentucky rifle, as it is called more popularly today), it was used extensively not only in those states but in Virginia, Maryland, the Carolinas, and throughout the southern colonies.

Pre-Revolutionary Pennsylvania rifles were a combination of the guns that preceded them. The barrel was long and slim like English or French fowlers and yet octagonal and rifled like

Mike Gahagan carving the buttstock of a fine Kentucky rifle.

the German Jaeger. There was a sliding wooden patch box on the buttstock to hold the cloth patches that were seated on top of the gunpowder. (A patch not only seals the gasses of the burning powder in a muzzleloader but ensures that the ball which is placed on top of it is engraved by the rifling so that it spins and is stabilized to ensure accuracy.)

During the Revolution the gun attained a legendary status for accuracy and helped stem the tide against the British at battles like Kings Mountain and Cowpens. In several skirmishes, while the British soldiers were standing in the open shooting their smoothbore Brown Bess muskets, which had an accuracy range of little more than seventy-five yards, Patriot riflemen were sniping from behind trees with deadly effectiveness at up to two hundred yards away.

During this time patchboxes fashioned out of brass began to appear, and more overall embellishment was seen. After the war and until the turn of the century the rifle became fancier and fancier until it evolved into what is called the golden age of the Kentucky rifle. A legend was born.

These incredible guns exhibited beautiful, swirling rococo relief carving, engraved patchboxes that had several openings or piercings to allow the gorgeous curly maple of the stock to show through, fine inlays of sterling silver wire, and small brass and silver figures including moons and stars.

The artisanship evident in these graceful guns is certainly one of the high points of American firearm craftsmanship and design, rivaled only by the wonderful double-barreled shotguns produced before World War II, and by today's exquisite custom classic stocked rifles.

While the long rifle was basking in its golden age, another distinctive form of Kentucky rifle was taking shape in the mountainous regions of the South. These Southern Kentuckys were much less elaborate, having browned (a controlled rusting process that turns the metal a deep brown and protects it, similar to bluing today) iron butt plates and trigger guards and sturdy but plain wood stocks. Instead of a stylish patchbox, many featured a simple tallow hole in the butt to keep bear grease or some other concoction handy for lubricating the patches. The rifles were less fancy, probably for two reasons: the natural resources of the region were more sparse and the customers of the country gunsmiths could neither afford nor did they want the frills that attracted patrons in the more affluent population centers. Calibers were larger than their eastern cousins to take care of hostile Indians and bears. Later these guns were also made into small caliber classic "squirrel rifles."

In the late 1700s and early 1800s pioneers continued to move westward over the Appalachians toward unexplored territories like "Caintuck" (where the gun gets its name). Many classic Kentucky and Southern rifles went along with these "Longhunters" to help explore and settle our country.

With the movement further and further west, new firearms showed up in the hands of the pioneers, like the Model 1803 U.S. Harpers Ferry rifled musket that accompanied Lewis and Clark on their monumental expedition to cross the Rockies to find a passage to the Pacific Ocean and the West Coast. Rifles for trade and treaty payments for the Indians were created by companies like Joseph Henry and Henry E. Leman. Simple, sturdy longrifles that served well in the tough conditions, these guns were also the most prevalent rifle used during the beginnings of the Fur Trade, from 1800 through about 1830.

The early mountainmen liked these tough, long-barreled flintlocks for their reliability (if you could find a hard rock to use in the lock, you could make the gun go off), but soon a new type began to appear on the western front which became known as the Plains rifle. It was ideally suited to the rigors of fur trapping, traveling by horseback, Indian and grizzly bear fighting, and buffalo and elk hunting. A Plains rifle was shorter and heavier of barrel (thirty to thirty-six inches compared to the over forty-inch barrel of longrifles), with large bores, generally of .50 to .54 caliber, and an extremely sturdy half stock. During this period the use of percussion caps began to replace flintlocks.

The most famous Plains rifle was created in the shop of two brothers, Sam and Jake Hawken, who worked in St. Louis, the jumping-off place for explorers heading west. The fame of the Hawken rifle's accuracy and reliability spread across the western half of the continent. It was relatively expensive for those days, though it usually had a plain maple stock with no patchbox and simple browned furniture. But it was so well designed that even though it normally weighed more than ten pounds, it carried and balanced like a fine English shotgun. Besides, the big gun shot straight and hard, the most important consideration in those perilous times.

Blackpowder muzzleloading firearms continued to be used as protection and for hunting well past the invention of the cartridge rifle. Their rich and varied history, with so many styles and superb examples of gunmaking, inspires today's custom gunsmiths to create masterpieces that would have made frontier gunsmiths and buckskinners envious.

To examine many of today's finest makers' work, make a trip to Friendship, Indiana, during the National Muzzleloading Rifle Association's annual rendezvous each summer. Exhibited there at the Gunmaker's Hall will be some of the finest craftsmanship being done in the world. The mountainmen would have jumped out of their buckskins to see such blackpowder-burning treasures.

Ordering a custom muzzleloader is as tradition bound as the guns themselves. Early in our country's history most firearms were essentially custom built, because colonial and frontier gunsmiths usually made a gun for a particular customer. There were no factories or production lines.

One such gunmaker, who is at the top of his craft, is Bob Harn of Venice, Florida. The southwestern corner of the Sunshine State might seem like a strange place for a blackpowder riflemaker, but Harn has been building fine muzzleloaders there for more than thirty years. He was a hardware store manager and built guns part time until 1984 when he went full time in the profession. His present-day guns reflect the influence of John Bivins, who is considered a modern master gunsmith (at this time he no longer makes guns but is busy doing restoration carving work on historic buildings).

Harn has become well known for making iron-mounted flint guns from the eighteenth century. Many times he antiques these rifles with a patina that makes them glow with the well-used luster of a trusted companion. They have a warm feeling about them with rounded edges and an "aged" metal finish that is very handsome.

Lately he has been building a wide variety of firearms, including golden age (1780-1790) rifles from Lancaster and York counties in Pennsylvania. He also makes Early American long rifles dating from 1760-1775, American (English-style) fowlers, late-period (1820-1840) squirrel rifles from the South, and a basic American-style pistol. For Germanic-gun admirers, he crafts Jaegers, a Germanic stalking rifle, and the German Flinte, a smoothbore fowling piece dating from 1730 to 1760.

Harn makes everything on the guns except their Siler locks and Getz barrels, both of which are considered by many to be the best. He assembles the locks from kits and cosmetically alters them to look like high-grade vintage English or German locks. Embellishments available are incise and relief carving, silver wire inlay work, patchboxes of wood or metal, handmade double-set triggers, hand-forged iron furniture, and several other custom additions. For example, you can have a longrifle made in four different grades, presently priced from $1,760 to $4,150 with other options carrying the price to $7,000 and above. You basically pay for the time spent to make the rifle more ornate. Within reason, if you want it, you can have it. Bob Harn is a complete and talented gunmaker.

I called Ron Ehlert of Duck River, Tennessee, recently, just as he returned from a successful blackpowder hunt. The rifle he used to take a nice six-point buck was a .54 caliber flintlock German-American transition longrifle he had made, a re-creation of rifles dated prior to the Revolutionary and French and Indian wars. Engraved on its buttstock are the words, in German, "Proud when in the hands of Master Ehlert, when at deer or elk aimed." On another part of the gun is the inscription, "Lucky is the animal who escapes me." You have got to like a fellow who hunts with a gun with that much character.

Since Ehlert is a German name, the craftsman feels he has roots back in the old country. In fact he now has on his books a couple of gun orders from German customers who have heard of his work. Other orders have placed his delivery time in the neighborhood of three years.

Ninety-nine percent of Ehlert's guns are American longrifle flintlocks in both Pennsylvania and Southern styles, along with selected English and German firearms. An artistic type, he has a degree in technical illustration and later worked in engineering for several companies. A full-time maker since 1984, he says he has been influenced in his gunmaking by Homer Dangler, John Bivins, and Monte Mandarino. Bob Harn is a close friend. Plain guns from his log cabin workshop start at $2,000 and go up from there with fine relief carving, wire inlay, and other additions. He has also now begun crafting engraved powder horns.

The town of Steadman, North Carolina, is more than three thousand miles from London, England. Yet, they share similar characteristics. From both you may order and acquire a bespoken shotgun of rare and superlative quality. In England the customer must go to historic firms like Purdey and Holland & Holland, and in Steadman you must seek out Mike Ehinger.

A blackpowder gunmaker for over thirty years, Ehinger is handcrafting some of the most exquisite firearms ever produced on these shores. He prefers to build English-style fowlers and double guns in the style of Manton and others who worked at the gun trade in London from 1790 to 1820. Those great gunmakers developed the two-barrel fowling pieces that were the forebearers of today's most admired and sought-after shotguns.

The craftsmanship evident in Ehinger's guns is extraordinary. Like the finest guns from across the big pond, his creations show the fantastic wood-to-metal fit that historically has been

An incredible Mike Ehinger totally handmade double-barreled English style flintlock fowler.

described as if "the metal grew in the wood." He makes everything on the guns, creating from scratch the watchlike quality locks, carving and meticulously oil-finishing the custom-fitted stocks from the finest European walnut, and hand-filing and boring the matched barrels. Such handwork takes a great deal of time, about one thousand hours per gun, so he can only build a couple of guns each year. Accordingly they cost about $20,000 each. Although at that price he certainly isn't getting rich, he is certainly following in a rich and proud tradition of gunmaking.

A personable gunmaker by the name of John Bergman lives in Puryear, Tennessee. He likes to build a variety of guns—from Jaegers to late-Hawken cartridge conversions from the 1840s. A full-time maker since 1976, his first gun was built from a Dixie Gun Works kit that he bought for one-hundred-fifty dollars and later sold for one-hundred-fifty dollars.

After a stint in the Navy and work in the seafood industry in Florida, Bergman began building Southern-style guns with Jack Garner, who ran a muzzleloading company in Tennessee. From there he started crafting guns under his own name and now produces about twenty per year. Delivery, depending on the gun ordered, can range from six months to a couple of years. His prices are very reasonable with an early-style Southern rifle going for about $900 and a Hawken for $1,500.

Jack Garner's Tennessee Valley Manufacturing is now located in Corinth, Mississippi, where he and a couple of associates still produce kits and custom muzzleloaders. Garner has been involved in the blackpowder business for thirty-two years. He spent fifteen years at Dixie Gun Works where he made guns, and then went full time in 1976. He is presently several months behind on his kit guns because of supply and demand and difficulty in getting the right parts; a custom gun will take about a year or longer. Kits sell for $550 to $650; customs are $1,250 and up.

Jim Chambers has been building custom muzzleloaders since 1970 when he began an apprenticeship under John Bivins at Old Salem in Winston-Salem, North Carolina. Now residing in Asheville, he produces kits and complete custom rifles and has recently purchased the Siler lock company. Silers are the lock of choice for most custom makers. A wide variety of styles are available from Chambers. He now has a young maker working for him by the name of Mike Gahagan who finishes some of Chambers's kits and builds a complete line of guns under his own name. Chambers's kits, which include a Siler lock, top quality Getz barrel, and finely precarved stock blank, cost $600. A finished, full-blown relief-carved rifle from Chambers can take two or more years to acquire, and run around $4,000. Gahagan's workmanship is excellent and his rifles are sure to appreciate. He makes a full line of eighteenth-century rifles and fowlers with prices from $1,500 to $5,000. A full-time maker for the past five years, he puts 200 to 225 hours of work into a scratch-built carved rifle.

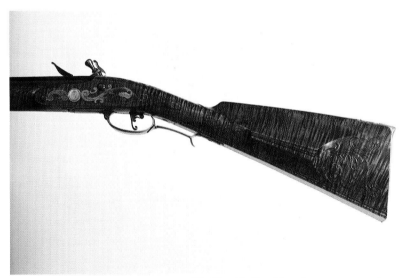

Carving and inlaying on a custom rifle like this Jim Chambers gun can take hundreds of hours.

Ted Hatfield of St. Joseph, Missouri, has been building what must be called a semicustom line of blackpowder rifles for some years now. His full-stocked squirrel rifle (Kentucky style) is made of the finest of components including AAA fancy curly maple stock. For the buckskinner who wants to shoot a beautiful muzzleloader just like Crockett and Boone did so long ago, but doesn't want to wreck his bank account, a Hatfield is the ticket. The long rifles presently sell for $820, slightly more for selected wood. Hatfield's new Mountain Rifle, which should be ready for shipment as you read this, is a half-stock Plains-style gun that should please anyone who wants to shoot or hunt with that type of rifle. It retails for $950.

Mankind has always had an artistic tendency, embellishing the tools we hunt with and even the weapons we use for war. From the times of cave drawings we have decorated spears, knives, guns, and almost any accessory connected to hunting.

One high point in this artistic legacy is the engraved powder horn, which had its golden age from roughly the 1750s to the mid-1780s. These powder horns, usually fashioned from a simple cow's horn to hold powder for flintlock rifles, had many historical variations and styles during the French and Indian War, Revolutionary War, and the Fur Trade. Within these styles came map horns (to show where a wanderer might have traveled in the frontier while exploring new country or during military campaigns), name horns (showing pride of ownership), and rhyme horns (to exhibit the poetic flair of its maker). Not only are these original powder horns valuable collector's items, but they are truly American works of art.

Gerald Dukes is an avid buckskinner-hornmaker in Waycross, Georgia, who specializes in beautiful re-creations of engraved (scrimshawed) horns. I saw Dukes's work a few years ago and immediately ordered a custom horn for myself. It is now a treasured family heirloom and a useful tool for shooting my flintlock. I believe that his horns are a tremendous bargain. The

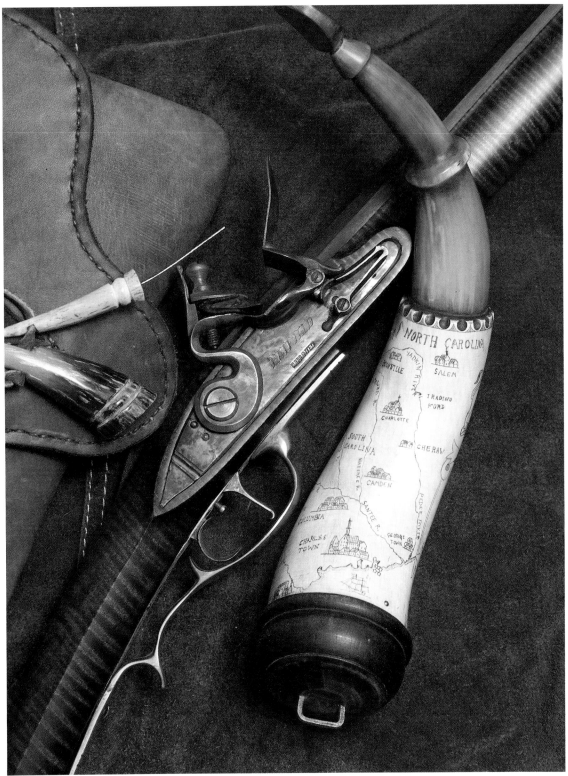

Gerald Dukes engraved (scrimshawed) powder horn and Ted Hatfield semicustom squirrel rifle.

fanciest, with full coverage engraving, cost only $200 to $300. Roughly one-fourth of that goes for materials. Considering it takes at least a month's work, he isn't going to get rich making horns. It is obviously a labor of love.

The engraving is done in a primitive style, similar to the best original horns. They have an antique finish and handcarved spout. I think it is incredible that such a beautiful creation, one that can become a most treasured possession, with history and heritage revealed in its craftsmanship, can cost only a couple of hundred dollars.

LONGBOWS & RECURVES

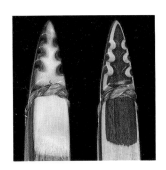

Bighorn longbow (left) is made with an impregnated maple handle and red elm limbs; the Jeffery recurve (right) features a zebrawood riser and maple limbs.

LONGBOWS & RECURVES

"So long as the new moon returns in heaven a bent, beautiful bow, so will the fascination of archery keep hold of the hearts of men."

Maurice Thompson in *The Witchery of Archery,* 1878

Once upon a time there was a mighty archer. A far-ranging and zealous hunter, he traveled afield with his trusted longbow and deadly arrows in search of new and challenging game. At last, he came upon his quarry, which strode arrogantly about, unaware of the brave huntsman.

Quietly, stealthfully, the hunter stalked the prey. Then the bow was drawn into its beautiful half-circle and the bolt unloosed, streaking straight as a dart to its mark. The arrow struck with great force and unerring accuracy. Our mighty archer triumphantly raised his bow high toward the heavens in thanks for a successful hunt.

Does this little story sound familiar? It should to many of us. It does to me because I was the archer—about seven or eight years old if I remember correctly. My conquest was a tall, rangy Rhode Island Red rooster that had been trying to spur me every time I went into my backyard. The chosen weapon was a hickory limb, scraped, dried, and fashioned into a bow with a string requisitioned from my mother's clothesline. Arrows were carefully straightened chinaberry limbs. The unlucky rooster, hit dead center, left the area with a great squawk and boil of ruffled feathers, dazed a bit but essentially unhurt. I had scored a bloodless coup but a coup nonetheless. (If my mother had found out about the clothesline or that I was shooting at her chickens, the day might not have been so triumphant.)

I'll bet almost every sportsman in America made his own bow and arrows as a child, whether to play cowboys and Indians or Robin Hood, or simply to experience the pure joy of using a bent stick and string to shoot another stick into the air.

Sadly, most of us forgot how much fun that was. The great majority of sportsmen graduated to firearms, or if they remained interested in archery, went from traditional bows to today's high-tech compound bows. I went the same route. After the lemonwood longbow I shot as a teenager finally broke, I bought one of the short recurves that were popular in the 1960s. Because of its length it was difficult to shoot accurately. It ended up in the attic. When compounds arrived on the scene I went through several, adding as many sight pins, silencers, and whatever else I could find to stick on them. Ultimately, they began gathering dust as well and I lost interest in archery.

Then several years ago I was reborn—an archer again. Advertisements for bowyers making longbows and recurves (or stick bows as they are sometimes called) began appearing more and more frequently in archery magazines. I had no idea at the time, but a groundswell of interest in traditional bows and arrows was occurring across the country. Maybe it would be fun to try a longbow again. I decided to investigate. From an ad for Dan Quillian's Archery Traditions I procured a longbow made of bam-

Appalachian Archery recurve (right) by Dave Guthrie with a beautiful sedua riser and curly maple limbs; longbow (left) with zircote handle and red elm limbs.

boo by Owen Jeffery, one of the best-known and respected bowyers in the country.

It was a thing of beauty, light in the hand and attractive to the eye. From the first shot I was in love again. A fifth of the weight of my compounds, it just felt like a bow should feel. Its almost musical "twung" as I released a cedar arrow sounded the way a bow should sound, quiet and strong.

Best of all, that first shot miraculously hit the target exactly where I was looking. I was a little shocked at first but then came the exhilaration known to all archers that have instinctively used their eyes and muscles to send an arrow to its mark.

Compounds, recurves, and longbows all certainly have their respective attributes. I currently shoot all three types and in the last year or so I have become more comfortable with today's compound. For the person not willing to spend the practice time required to master a traditional bow they are easier to use to ensure a clean kill in hunting situations. A modern compound is like a benchrest rifle, deadly accurate in experienced hands, though shooting errors are magnified when using one, as when, for example, a hunter is forced to shoot from an awkward position.

A finely made recurve with its graceful limbs is to some eyes the most beautiful of bows. It is relatively stable and is easier to shoot well than a longbow, especially for someone used to compounds or someone who is making the transition to traditional archery.

The half-moon arc of a longbow when at full draw is simple and elegant. It is the most stable bow, with shooting qualities that are forgiving of a bad release or a breakdown in form. Perhaps most important, one generally *likes* a compound, while a treasured recurve or longbow is *loved*.

Indeed, there is a revival of interest in traditional archery sweeping the country. A good example is the Great Lakes Longbow Invitational shoot held in Michigan each summer. I attended recently, and if anyone has any doubts about the resurgence of traditional archery they should have been there. It is strictly a straight-end bow and wood-arrow event, yet more than 6,000 people were in attendance. I met archers from Sweden, Canada, France, and throughout the U.S. The competitive events attracted a phenomenal 1,679 shooters, with 110 dealers selling traditional tackle, and over 1,000 folks camped on the premises. No, traditional archery is not a fad, it is a vibrant, fast-growing movement.

A couple of years ago when I attended the World Longbow Championship in Wilsonville, Alabama, I saw all sorts of shooters—from a priest to an airline pilot, from a chemist to a minister—all having a great time.

That the straight-end longbow gives such satisfaction comes as no surprise. It is the most venerable weapon of all time. During the past five hundred centuries it has been a trusted implement of hunting and warfare for Stone Age *Homo sapiens,* aboriginal natives, medieval foot soldiers, and today's sportsmen. The recurve is much younger, about four thousand years old, and the compound is only a quarter of a century old.

The longbow, before the atomic bomb and the era of the firearm, was the most devastating weapon on earth.

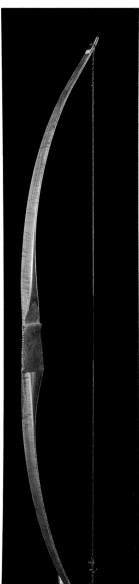

Guthrie flatbow with gorgeous curly maple limbs and highly figured cocobolo handle is reminiscent of the bows used by the American Plains Indians.

In medieval times the English yeoman's longbow of stout yew was the main tool in England's dominance of Europe and the beginnings of the British Empire. Since the English soldier could shoot a steel-tipped arrow into the air every five seconds to distances of over two hundred yards, a regiment of five thousand archers could produce a horrible rain of sixty thousand deadly projectiles per minute in warfare! The three most famous examples of the longbow's superiority were the battles with France at Crecy, Poitiers, and Agincourt.

At Crecy in 1346, the English—with four thousand men-at-arms, ten thousand longbowmen, and five thousand foot troops—defeated a French army of twelve thousand horsemen, six thousand crossbowmen, and twenty thousand foot troops. Several thousand French were killed including fifteen hundred knights and members of the aristocracy. Just fifty Englishmen were killed. With its speed of fire and great range the English longbow was more than a match for the French crossbow.

In 1356 at Poitiers, six thousand Englishmen defeated nearly three times that number of French. A small group of longbowmen repelled every French attack. When the battle was over, two thousand French knights and nobles were killed, several thousand foot soldiers left dead, and many troops captured including the French king and his son.

Around forty thousand French attacked the ten thousand English at Agincourt in 1415. The six thousand longbowmen devastated the French. With fewer than two hundred British killed (some sources say fewer than twenty-five) the French dead numbered many thousands including over five thousand noblemen, almost destroying the aristocracy of France. With the coming of firearms in the 1500s, the longbow was gradually displaced as a weapon of warfare in Europe.

From this most illustrious period we got the legend of Robin Hood, perhaps the most famous and beloved outlaw in history. A bold figure of resistance to tyranny, he fought evil Prince

John Schultz all-bamboo longbow and osage Appalachian Archery bow backed with copperhead snakeskin.

John and the dastardly Sheriff of Nottingham to restore Good King Richard the Lionhearted to the throne. Whether true or not, it is a wonderful story even today and has been the subject of scores of motion pictures and television shows.

Also from this romantic time we retain many expressions pertaining to archery that have become part of the English language: *yeoman's service* (unfailing devotion), *high strung* (under great tension), brace yourself (get ready for action), and others like *straight as an arrow, point blank, bolt upright, keep tab, rule of thumb, to be the butt* (target of something unpleasant like an arrow or practical joke), and *bolt from the blue* (where an arrow came from during a battle).

Although we owe much of our archery heritage to pioneers like Saxon Pope and Art Young and Will and Maurice Thompson, perhaps the most important date in archery history for the American sportsman might be November 13, 1899. It was then that a southern gentleman named Howard Hill was born on a cotton plantation in Shelby, Alabama. One of the most influential figures in all of American sport, Howard Hill is truly the patron saint of bowhunting and archery in the United States. He is considered by many to be the greatest archer/bowhunter that ever lived. Using his bamboo-cored longbows in the 1930s, 1940s, and 1950s, he was really responsible for advancing bowhunting in the U.S. His book *Hunting the Hard Way* is a classic, as are his many movies and short films like *Tembo,* shot on location in Africa.

Howard Hill's accomplishments are legendary. A man of incredible strength who could string a one-hundred-pound bow while sitting down, he was the first white man to kill an elephant with a bow and arrow. He won 196 field archery tournaments in a row, took two thousand head of game, developed the Howard Hill broadhead still used today by many traditional archers, and did countless shooting exhibitions all over the world including shooting coins out of the air. Hill was the star of twenty-three short subjects for Warner Brothers and did all of the trick shots in the 1937 production of *Robin Hood* starring Errol Flynn. His legacy is a strong force in traditional archery today.

Fred Bear, a lanky fellow from Grayling, Michigan, was perhaps the most famous bowhunter of all time. With recurves designed by him and built by the company that still bears his name, he was a pioneer in bowhunting big game all over the globe. He also popularized the sport by way of movies and TV. A generation of sportsmen marveled at Bear's exploits on his trips to Africa for lion, elephant, and Cape buffalo, to India for Bengal tiger, and to Alaska for his world-record Kodiak bear and polar bear.

Even after compounds had become the rage in bowhunting, Fred Bear still used his beloved recurves with his instinctive style of shooting. And indeed it is instinctive shooting that draws many

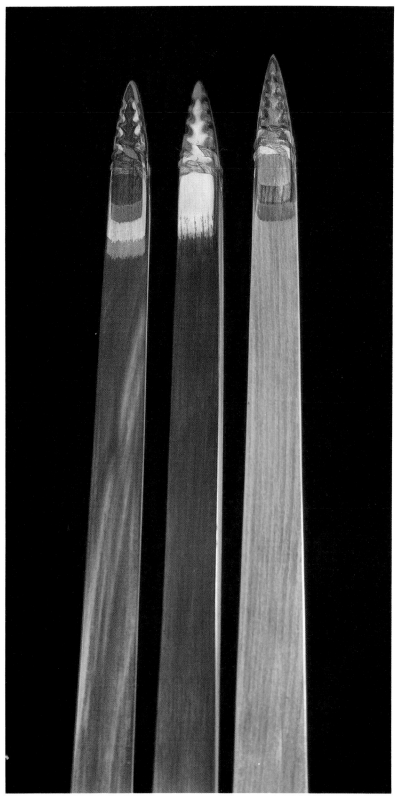

Custom bows can be crafted from many different materials; examples shown here include (from left) red cedar limb with osage tip overlay, zebrawood with bighorn sheep horn tip, and osage with cocobolo.

of today's traditionalists to the longbow and recurve. They firmly believe that these bows, shot instinctively, are a more effective hunting tool. A longbow, and to a lesser degree a recurve, are above all stable, with shooting qualities that are forgiving of a bad release or breakdown in form.

The instinctive style, with no sights, uses the brain (as an instant problem-solving computer), muscle memory, and eye-hand coordination to achieve successful shots on moving game.

There is only one drawback to traditional archery. Or rather it is a requirement and commitment. It takes many hours of practice before the archer can shoot well enough to go hunting. It takes dedication to build the physical strength to draw heavy hunting bows. If the hunter is not willing to pay his dues then the compound, with its weight reduction and precise sighting system, is the way to go. However, as one who has gone full circle with all types of bows, I am having more fun now that I have rediscovered the longbow and recurve.

One of the great pluses in the revival of traditional archery today is the proliferation of custom bowyers, arrow makers, and companies crafting some of the finest equipment ever. Robin Hood would have been proud! And, getting outfitted with a handmade bow and accessories is relatively inexpensive compared to the prices of firearms. Well-made longbows and recurves can be obtained for as little as $150 to $600.

Sportsmen interested in a longbow from an individual or factory must first decide what type of bow and what material it is to be made from. Longbows are made in two ways. Self bows are made of a single piece of wood, like yew or osage. Composite laminated bows have outer layers of fiberglass sandwiched over several tapered laminations of wood such as maple, osage, bamboo, red elm, cedar, and yew.

If you ask ten makers what type of material is best you will probably get ten different answers. It is really a matter of personal preference, but each has its different qualities. For example, osage is a tough wood with excellent cast (ability to throw an arrow). Usually bright yellow when it is first cut, it mellows with exposure to sunlight to a lovely amber color. It is a superior wood for self bows. Yew, the old standby, is a rich coppery color and makes a fast, sweet-shooting bow, while red elm has several good attributes and is probably the most popular wood used today for laminated bows. Bamboo, actually a species of grass, makes a great-shooting bow and has the nostalgic value of being the same material Howard Hill used in his famous bows.

Another decision is whether to get a narrow, deep-cored longbow or a flatbow or recurve. Deep-core bows are generally long (sixty-four to seventy inches), like those used by English yeoman, while flatbows are wider and shorter (sixty to sixty-four inches) emulating their predecessors, the bows of Native Americans. The longer lengths tend to be stable, forgiving, and fast, especially if they are one of the reflex-deflex designs, and the flatbows exhibit good speed and are great for tree stands and thick hunting conditions.

Recurves are usually in the sixty- to sixty-four-inch range and are fast

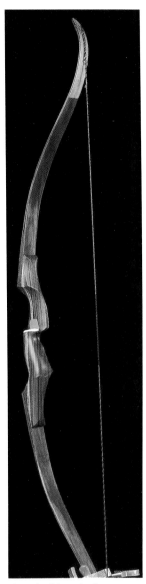

Appalachian Archery recurve with zebrawood limbs and pau ferro riser.

and comfortable to shoot. Few sporting items approach their simple beauty and graceful lines. They are generally a bit faster than longbows, although longbows are catching up, and they have less hand shock than the straight-end sticks. Many recurves are built in a takedown design which makes them ideal for the traveling bowhunter.

Most archery shops are primarily devoted to the sale of compounds, but they may stock or can order factory traditional bows from companies like Martin, Bear, Pearson, and several others. However, there are talented custom makers scattered across the country for the sportsman who desires handmade qualities in his equipment.

One name that is at the top of the list is Fred Anderson of Grapeview, Washington. His craftsmanship and beautiful finish work are admired both by his clients and other bowyers. A school-teacher who builds part time, ten to twenty hours a week and longer during the summer, he laughs when asked about the success of his bowmaking.

"Well, I'm a professional. I've been building bows since 1963. It's knowledge really," he says. "I worked my way through college making bows. I've made thousands. I use a core of pre-stressed maple and tapered fiberglass and a lot of handwork. But I also believe it's an art form and an artist should bring out the best in his work."

A deer and elk hunter, Anderson is clear on why he chose to stick with the longbow. "Shooting a longbow gives you a sense of self-fulfillment. It is an athletic adventure for which you must train your muscles. You are are using your own wits and wisdom to shoot the bow rather than technical achievement as with the compound."

In the hills of West Virginia, a personable bowyer named Dave Guthrie runs his one-man shop called Appalachian Archery. He does all aspects of bowmaking, from cutting his own trees, sawing the laminations, and spraying the final finish to making

Longbows by (from left) Bobby Lofton, Chuck Jones, and Fred Anderson.

the Flemish-style string. On all of his models he uses clear fiberglass to allow the natural beauty of the hardwoods to show through. For core woods he uses the prettiest osage I've ever seen, as well as cedar, zebrawood, red elm, and maple.

Guthrie builds two deep-core longbows, one reflexed and the other reflex-deflex, two flatbows, two beautiful takedown recurves, and two one-piece recurves. One recurve has a longbow-type handle reminiscent of the great bows of the 1950s, and the other model features a handle similar to the recurves popular in the 1960s. Each customer's bow is custom made, one at a time.

I have been shooting an extraordinarily handsome osage longbow by Guthrie this past season. It is sweet shooting and puts an arrow where I look. Its limbs are a deep reddish brown with copperhead snakeskins covering the back, and the handle is top-quality cocobolo. Recently I took delivery of a gorgeous takedown recurve with a super piece of zebrawood for the riser and curly maple limbs. It is a striking piece of work and shoots as good as it looks.

Guthrie is committed to giving his customers the best for their money. "I realize a custom bow is a major investment and I will do whatever is necessary to ensure your complete satisfaction," the bowyer says with conviction. He is also dedicated to traditional archery. "Appalachian Archery was founded in 1985 on the belief that bowhunting should be more than speed and advertising hype. I felt bows should be simpler and have an aesthetic value as well as being able to humanely dispatch any animal you pursue." An accomplished bowhunter with many trophies to his credit, Guthrie makes beautiful bows that work well. Appalachian bows are reasonably priced and reflect superb craftsmanship on a par with any others.

In the past decade bowyers Jerry Brumm and Rick Shepard have brought their company, Great Northern Longbow Company, to the forefront of traditional equipment. One of the first makers to produce a superior flatbow of native-grown hardwoods

Owen Jeffery shows that custom bow manufacture requires a great deal of hand work.

such as osage and red elm, their Bushbow is the one by which others are judged. Like their short longbow, the Critter Gitter, it is a reflex-deflex design for smooth draw and little hand shock. They also make a deep core traditional longbow and two models of one-piece recurves. Several of their bows are available in a unique hinged model called the Jack Knife Series that folds for ease of transport. All Great Northern bows feature their trademark small torque-free handle and have twelve coats of a catalyzed finish that is impervious to moisture. For craftsmanship and appeal to the bowhunter they are hard to beat.

Montana has become a haven for traditional bowyers in recent years because of its ideal dry climate for bowmaking and its great deer and elk hunting. One of the brightest stars in Big Sky Country is Dick Robertson of Lewistown, whose Stykbows are considered among the best on the market.

He builds a complete line of longbows, flatbows, and recurves in a number of different core woods including red elm and bamboo that he tempers just as rodmakers do their split-cane fly rods. Robertson even faces several models with an optional snakeskin backing of Montana rattler or Texas diamond-back.

The words "master bowyer" describe no person better than Owen Jeffery. He is best known for his recurves, although he and his son Tom make a number of fine longbows. Certainly no one in history has made more bows. To date, Jeffery has personally used his bowmaking skill to produce more than an astounding fifty thousand bows! In addition, he has overseen the making of virtually hundreds of thousands of traditional bows, more than any living bowyer.

Beginning in 1949, he worked as a bowyer for Hoyt for sixteen years and was the bow designer when the company developed its famous Pro Medalist, the competition recurve of its day, and many of their other models. While at Bear Archery for $7\frac{1}{2}$ years, Jeffery was the bowyer and vice president of manufacturing, redesigning all the Bear recurves in 1967. From 1973 to 1976 he ran the Shakespeare archery operation and then started his own company in Columbia, South Carolina, where he works today.

He is still one of the hardest-working men I've ever seen. At sixty-eight years old he looks and acts like a man fifteen years younger. "I retired three years ago," he says with a devilish gleam in his eyes. "I've cut down to about fourteen hours a day now."

While he, Tom, and a small group of craftsmen make longbows and recurves for several private labels as well as their own, not too many folks realize that Owen will also personally handcraft a custom bow for customers at extremely attractive prices. (Approximately half what a couple of other well-known companies charge for their bows.)

His standard line of bows are really factory built, although they are made by hand like all bows. He also makes his custom bows for individuals exactly like any other maker, including, at

Two generations of bowyers: Tom Jeffery shooting longbow and Owen Jeffery with recurve.

times, even using handforms. Jeffery custom recurves are on a par with any made by anybody, and in many cases better. Delivery time on both recurves and longbows is among the shortest in the industry.

John Schulz is a living legend. Along with his sons, the longbow pioneer from Canby, California, makes the Stradivarius of longbows. They craft what they call the American Longbow, which is an all-wood laminated bow backed with bamboo. Unlike laminated bows that have fiberglass backing and facings, the Schulz longbow follows the string (retains a slightly bent shape toward the direction of the string), which he feels makes for more accuracy and the smoothest, sweetest-shooting bow possible. Core woods are osage, hickory, and, on special order, yew. There is an all-bamboo model as well. All are simply elegant, with the highest quality craftsmanship one can imagine.

They, like their creator, are destined to become part of our American archery heritage. Actually, John Schulz, a youthful sixty-three years old, has already secured his place in the hierarchy of bow and arrow history. He was a protege of the great Howard Hill and gained much of his knowledge of traditional archery from him. The result is the ultimate Hill-style bow very similar to longbows Hill made in the early part of his career. If an archer wants a great-shooting bow with superb workmanship and one that will be a treasured addition to his collection of sporting equipment, a Schulz longbow is the ultimate archery possession.

I think every fan of traditional archery, whether he is eight years old or three-quarters of a century, is transported back to the days of Robin Hood when he shoots a wooden arrow into the air. Our forest-green-clad hero undoubtedly used a stout bow of good yew with a reddish brown heartwood belly and white sapwood back.

On Prince of Wales Island, Ketchikan, Alaska, from the shop of Gerald Welchman, you may attain such a bow. He specializes in English longbows made of the finest Oregon yew. His prized stock of wood was cut on the slopes of the Cascades in 1988, by the bowyer himself, at elevations between 3,000 and 4,700 feet. These bows are beautifully made and as Welch says, "must perform to my standards. These bows must be quick of cast, comfortable to shoot, reliable, and good looking. They also must be a bow that I would like to own myself. I do not send out any less." Welchman longbows, considering the craftsmanship, are very reasonably priced.

Can you get a great longbow from a farmer? Yes, you can, if you order a Blackhawk Bow from Jack Smith of Princeton, Illinois. His lineup of longbows includes a traditional straight reflex, a reflex-deflex, and a flatbow. They are built of osage, red elm, sassafras, and red cedar, with walnut, black locust, maple, yew, and bamboo also available. Except for yew and bamboo, Smith cuts most of the wood right there in the Midwest. Because of the seasonal nature of farming he has plenty of time to search out exceptional materials and to make his bows. And since he hasn't been building them for too many years, even though they are finely crafted, his prices put them in the bargain category.

Ed Barwick and Dale Anderson are partners in Shawnee Traditions in Marion, Illinois. They make a complete line of excellent longbows, flatbows, and recurves. In addition they also offer a "Li'l Hunter" 56-inch longbow for young archers.

Paul Fox of Sandy, Oregon, builds a takedown longbow that has always intrigued me. A reflex-deflex design, it has a stainless steel sleeve with a brass insert which essentially breaks the bow into two parts. When joined the bow looks like it is one piece, and the slight additional weight in the handle section actually helps its performance. It sure would be a great bow to have on those long-distance hunting trips when equipment must be carried in small vehicles and even smaller airplanes. Fox also makes one-piece longbows and a lovely takedown recurve with a tremendous selection of fancy handle materials.

While roving the shooting grounds of the Great Lakes Longbow Invitational, I spied several archers shooting exceptionally pretty longbows with gorgeous laminations. Upon closer examination I saw they were the work of J.D. Berry of Spokane, Washington. The handles had multiple laminations of various hardwoods and on some, the limbs featured pinstriped laminations running tip to tip. Their owners seemed to think that they were exceptional shooters as well.

Osage wood has been prized by American archers for centuries. Indians searched it out wherever it grew as the bow wood of choice. The French called it "bois d' arc" or "wood of the bow." It is labeled by some as hedge apple, or "bowdark," but regardless it is one of my favorite woods. With a bow made of it I always feel as if I could head out into the wilderness on an extended hunting trip or an arrow-slinging medieval fracas and depend on my bow not to fail me. Chuck Jones, of Vandalia,

Illinois, makes a great osage longbow. His company is called Okaw Valley Longbows, and the top-of-the-line bow is called the Osage Royal. Other core woods may be ordered.

Harry Elburg's bows have achieved quite a reputation in the Midwest and across the nation. He makes straight-end bows and recurves in his Madison, Indiana, shop that are known for exceptional speed and fine workmanship. Archers shooting Elburg bows have won a number of longbow competitions. The bows are very fairly priced. Elburg also invented the Grizzly broadhead for traditional hunters. It is designed to be sharpened with only a file and has a single beveled edge. During one independent test the Grizzly proved to give more penetration than any other broadhead. Elburg has turned the broadhead production over to another firm so he can concentrate on the demand for his bows.

Jim Brackenbury was a well-liked and respected bowyer in Gresham, Oregon, until his tragic accidental death a couple of years ago. Now his company goes on, with superb longbows and recurves still coming from the Oregon township. They add new meaning to the word "custom" with core materials like yew, osage, or red elm, and riser handles from osage, cocobolo, zebrawood, wenge, tulip, bocote, shedua, purpleheart, bubinga, walnut, or any combination of such woods. Tip overlays are deer antler, elk, moose, caribou, stag, bighorn sheep, Dall sheep, musk ox, Cape buffalo, and baleen whale.

When it comes to continuing a tradition, no company has enjoyed a longer run of producing great longbows than the Howard Hill Archery Company in Hamilton, Montana. It is run by Craig Ekin, who learned from his father, Ted Ekin, a business associate of Hill's, and from the man himself. He makes the complete line of Hill bows and is developing a number of new models and limited editions.

The Bighorn Bowhunting Company, in Lupton, Colorado, and its great recurves and longbows were the creations of G. Fred Asbell. One of the most outspoken and popular disciples of traditional archery, Asbell is a fervent advocate of its values and is past president of the Pope and Young Club. Bighorns are now made by King of the North, but Asbell remains as an advisor. These distinctive bows are known for superb workmanship and top performance. I shoot a Bighorn longbow regularly, and it is one of the best I've ever used for speed, smoothness, and almost no hand shock.

The Black Widow Custom Bow Company of Highlandville, Missouri, has been making top-quality recurves since 1957. One of the few companies that continued to make only recurves after the compound hit the market, Black Widow introduced a new longbow last year. All of their bows feature Fast Flex limbs and Fast Flight strings (a new low-stretch material used by some bowyers for more speed than traditional Dacron). Black Widows have a devoted following among knowledgeable bowhunters.

John Strunk, of Tillamook, Oregon, handcrafts some of the most traditional bows of all, self English longbows of Pacific yew and flatbows of osage. He also makes laminated longbows of a number of different woods with very traditional styling. His Spirit Longbow Company products are finely made and extremely reasonably priced considering the time and handwork involved in their construction.

Probably no one in the country is more active in the promotion of traditional archery than Dan Quillian, who owns Archery Traditions in Athens, Georgia. He is certainly the most outspoken in his love of the sport. His enthusiasm is almost a crusade to convert sportsmen to the longbow and recurve.

Quillian knows what he's talking about because he is constantly field-testing equipment. A couple of years ago he and his son went to Africa on a longbow safari. They took eleven game animals including bushbuck, gemsbok, and eland. On the moose-sized eland he got complete penetration, something the outfitter had never seen with compounds. He recently took a record Alaskan coastal grizzly with one shot. The bear, arrowed at close range, just flinched at the shot and walked away, piling up less than 200 yards away. Because of the quietness of the longbow the 8½-foot grizzly never knew the bowhunter was in the neighborhood.

Most of the Georgian's trophies have been taken with his Longhunter bamboo or red elm-cored longbow, a model that he designed and is built by top bowyers. He also has a new one-piece recurve called the Canebrake and a takedown called the Patriot. One of his favorite digs at compound shooters is to ask jokingly, "When are you going to take those training wheels off your bow?"

The lure of traditional archery—with the sweet hum of the string on a handcrafted longbow or recurve and the glow of beautiful, polished hardwoods—takes hold of all those who rediscover its magic. With an increasing number of bowyers, arrow makers, bowhunters, and just folks who like to watch the flight of an arrow propelled from a simple and elegant piece of equipment, this centuries-old form of outdoor pleasure is sure to grow and remain strong in the hearts of men.

DECOY
CARVINGS

A carving in process by Larry Hayden, a pioneer in realistic wood sculpture.

DECOY
CARVINGS

There is something immensely soul-satisfying about carving on a piece of wood with a sharp knife. It is a statement of creative expression that seems to be pure and unfettered, whether the artist is a 10-year-old boy whittling on a stick with his Boy Scout knife, or a world-class carver putting the intricate finishing touches on a masterpiece sculpture priced in the six figure range.

The thinly cut shavings that give way to the sharpened blade and the smell of the wood as it is sliced and shaped into the form of a graceful bird is a powerful attraction to those who choose the avocation.

Carving decoys to attract waterfowl is an original American art form. It can be traced back to a 1,000-year-old Indian counterfeit bird found in a cave in Nevada. The sole purpose of this decoy was to put ducks, geese, and swans in the pot. Undoubtedly it also gave its creator a great deal of satisfaction. The golden age of the wooden duck began after the banning of the live decoys in the 1930s. This led market gunners and other innovative duck hunters to fashion wooden deceivers to lure the birds into range of their scatterguns.

In the last couple of decades those hard-working American waterfowlers have been exalted as true artists, and their creations have sometimes fetched unbelievable amounts of money from enthusiastic collectors. Names like Elmer Crowell, Ira Hudson, Harry Shourds, Shang Wheeler, Joel Barber, Madison Mitchell, Benjamin Holmes, Charles Perdew, Ben Schmidt, Mitchell La Frances, and Lem and Steve Ward have taken their place in the history of American folk art.

Those noteworthy decoy carvers came from places found on the Atlantic Flyway—the Susquehanna Flats on the northern end of Chesapeake Bay; Cobb Island, Virginia; Chincoteague Island, Virginia; and other coastal areas in Maine, Massachusetts, Michigan, New Jersey, Connecticut, Maryland, and Louisiana located on the Central Flyway.

Sportsmen's fascination with the hand-carved hunting decoy is reflected in the prices they have paid for some premier examples, at times in excess of $100,000! An Elmer Crowell decoy sold in the mid-1980s for the astronomical sum of $319,000.

While the interest in collecting these historical birds was reaching a fever pitch, another form of carving was gaining in popularity and approaching its zenith in artistic expression. Decorative carvings (at first ducks, but now all sorts of birds and other wildlife), as they are crafted today, are unbelievably realistic. You almost expect them to fly away.

A superb decorative carving pays homage to the beauty of wildfowl. Each feather is carved with precision. The feathers stand out in relief, yet exhibit a feeling for the softness of the bird. The artist must be an excellent designer to formulate the layout of how the bird is sitting, looking, or flying. He or she must be a master wood carver to show the detail of the feathers and exhibit a knowledge of anatomy. And finally the carving must be skill-fully painted, showcasing the glorious palette of colors that nature bestowed upon waterfowl. Indeed, painting may be the most difficult aspect of all, to capture the iridescent green head of a drake mallard, the earthy and subtle browns of a gadwall, or the brilliant spectrum of a drake wood duck.

Woods like basswood, white cedar, white and sugar pine, and tupelo are used for their carvability. Some artists working in a more interpretive style may even extract a dynamic, flowing sculpture out of a single log of hardwood. The carver may use a simple pocketknife or a series of treasured handmade carving

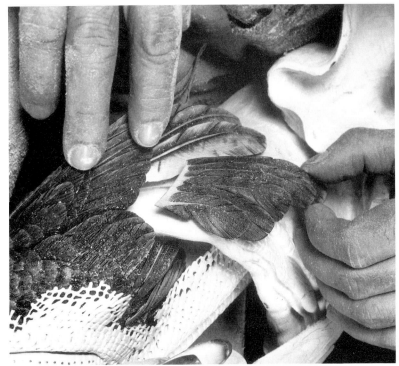

Ted Borg

The carving of individual feathers was pioneered by artists like Grainger McKoy.

Grainger McKoy carving of a woodcock bursting from cover.

McKoy assembling the intricate construction of his carving of flying ducks.

knives, designed and precisely ground for different functions in the carving process. Large portions of material are taken off the block of wood by band saws, hand grinders, flexible shaft machines, power carvers, and sanding drums. Of course, good old-fashioned elbow grease and a copious supply of sandpaper is also needed.

The burning of feather detail is painstakingly done with a fine-tipped instrument that incises each vein of each feather—a process that can take hundreds of hours, as can the final painting.

As unlikely a place as an oysterhouse located in Beaufort, South Carolina, was the birthplace of a particular style of dynamic wood sculpture. Two men, Gilbert Maggioni, who owned the seafood establishment, and Grainger McKoy, his younger friend and hunting companion, were both waterfowlers and carvers of wooden birds. They decided that they could carve better, more realistic birds than the ones they had seen at a carving exhibition held on Maryland's Eastern Shore.

Maggioni was soon carving ducks that were actually flying, not just sitting on the water. McKoy followed his lead and both began to design fantastic, intricately carved and assembled works of art. One of Maggioni's more well-known sculptures is of two pintail drakes bursting from the surface of the water. Individual feathers were carved with fine detail and inserted into the piece to give it life and a powerful feeling of movement. Habitat was included with these carvings, and sometimes several birds were linked by only their wing tips, beaks, or the tips of their feet.

McKoy began developing carvings that were simply not previously within the realm of anyone's imagination. He had found his life's work and a medium of expression that would take him to the pinnacle of wood sculpture. Several of his most memorable pieces still boggle the mind in their artistry and complexity. One depicted three marsh hens fighting in midair over a small

Grainger McKoy's incredible carving of a covey rise of thirteen bobwhite quail blasting from cover.

Ted Borg

fish. Another portrayed a wren landing in an old boot filled with nesting material. One of my favorites was a single woodcock jumping from the ground, its wings fully extended downward in its initial leap.

As McKoy carved he worked out more and more complicated and demanding designs to challenge himself and the medium. He created whole flocks of teal slipping into the decoys, their wings ripping the air as they descended. Perhaps his most famous sculpture is called *Covey Rise*. It features thirteen bobwhite quail bursting from cover, each suspended from another's wing tips. That phenomenal work took almost two years to complete. A quiet, unassuming man who is considered one of the most innovative artists in the world, McKoy is presently still at work in South Carolina, producing new and even more challenging sculptures.

In 1993 at the Ward World Championship Wildfowl Carving Competition (held each year by the Ward Foundation in Salisbury, Maryland) names like Larry Barth, Pat Godin, Jim Sprankle, John T. Sharp, and one or more of the Brunets (Tan and his two sons Jett and Jude) were seen on the winning entries, as they have been many times before. Their work is extraordinary.

Larry Barth, of Stahstown, Pennsylvania, won the Best in World Decorative Lifesize Wildfowl category with a sculpture of a least bittern and a marsh wren perched on a small grouping of cattails. He won for the fourth time since he took the championship in 1985.

Pat Godin of Brantford, Ontario, has been at the top level of wood sculpture since he first won the World Championship for Decorative Pairs in 1976 with a super carving of a drake and hen goldeneye. He was only twenty-three years old at the time. This past year his carving of a grouse took third place in Decorative Lifesize. Over the years he has become known for beautifully designed and executed duck carvings. In 1982 a carving of a pair

A pair of preening pintails exhibit Pat Godin's incredibly detailed carving techniques.

Brian Barrer

Godin's Birch Lake—Ruffed Grouse.

Brian Barrer

Pat Godin is considered one of the world's finest carvers.

of black ducks took Best in World, this time with the ducks hissing at a still-wet muskrat in a marsh setting. Another pairs championship came in 1983 with an innovative sculpture entitled *Nuptial Aggression—American Widgeons.*

For the past several years Godin has been carving more upland birds and other nonduck subjects like his fantastic *Black Bellied Magpie and Deer Mouse,* which won Best in Show at the 1983 North American Wildfowl Carving Competition and at the 1984 International Wildfowl Carving Exhibition. It is plain to see that any time he enters a competition he is one of the favorites.

Godin's knowledge of bird anatomy has been one of the key ingredients in his carvings. He holds a Master of Science degree in wildlife ecology and does a great deal of study before starting a piece.

Tan Brunet carving of a merganser head reflects his dramatic Cajun style of wood sculpture.

Carl Danos's smooth canvasback represents the zenith in unburned working decoys.

"Good design is what separates good work from the best work," he says. "The carving must have movement and dynamics. That's why I work out my designs in clay before starting to carve. It is more spontaneous, like an artist's quick sketch, only in three dimensions."

He also studies live birds, not only close to his Canadian home, but also down in Louisiana where he and his wife, Jessica, first met. For some years after he started carving, and still today, he makes the trek down south to see the wintering birds and visit with the best of the Cajun carvers. His background is French Canadian and he naturally was attracted to the work of the great carvers of the bayou country. He became friends with Tan Brunet and Jimmy Vizier, both top competitive carvers. Vizier's father, Odee, was a commercial decoy carver of great repute whose work is now very collectible. Jimmy is one of the best competitive gunning decoy carvers in the world and ultimately became Godin's father-in-law when Pat married his daughter.

Godin now does three types of carvings. His most complex competition works, of which he does about two a year, currently sell for around $40,000, and his single realistic birds go for $10,000 to $20,000. He has also started carving "smoothies" (unburned decoys) that cost from $1,000 to $3,000. Because of his many championships he has also found great demand for his three books on carving and patterns; his synthetic study birds, molded with great detail; a video; and even a line of paintbrushes.

Down in Galliano, Louisiana, in Bayou Lafourche, there reigns a family of royalty among world-class decoy carvers. It is the monarchy of the King of the Cajun Carvers, Tan Brunet and his two sons, Jett and Jude.

Tan Brunet has won the World Championship in Floating Pairs an unprecedented five times; Jett Burnett has won it twice. This past year Jude Brunet won the 1993 Best in World Floating Decorative Lifesize Waterfowl Pair with a gorgeous twosome of ring-necked ducks. In the Open Level of the Ward Championships, Jett won first and second place in Decorative Lifesize Floating Waterfowl, first in Marsh ducks and first in Mallards, Diving Ducks and Scaup. The Brunet aristocracy continues to rule the decoy world.

The elder statesman of the Brunet clan began to carve in the 1960s as an offshoot of his duck hunting. The Acadian heritage of harvesting the fruit of the land was strong in his desire to make decoys to put food on his family's table. He would get together to carve ducks with many of his friends including Jimmy Vizier, a relative. His work got better and better until he won the pairs competition for the first time in 1977. Since then he has introduced several innovations to the craft including his three-dimensional remarques of miniature ducks and an integrated counterweight system designed right in the decoy. He established the Brunet name as an icon in decoy carving. His sons were obviously paying attention.

Seven miles south of where Tan Brunet plys his craft, another Cajun carver is producing beautiful birds in the tradition of the old masters. Carl Danos of Lockport, Louisiana, has become known for his magnificent working-style decoys. Although he carves excellent decorative decoys with each feather exhibiting intricately burned detail, his "smoothies" or gunning birds are extraordinary. I first saw them at a show and even though the room was filled with wonderful examples of elaborate wood sculpture, Danos's creations were among the most compelling. They have the familiar fat, healthy style prevalent in some Cajun carvers' work, with beautiful painting and sculpting.

Like many Louisiana-based artists, Danos and his brother Reagan, who is also a wood carver, come from a family that has always been close to the land and its hunting heritage. "Our family, and especially my Dad, lived off the land," Danos says. "He trapped, oystered, and was a trawler fisherman. A lot of us that lived up and down the bayou did the same."

That is why the bayou country of Louisiana has been a

Dramatic wood sculpture of pheasants by Jim Robinson.

Robinson carving of gyrfalcon shows his expert knowledge of raptor anatomy.

hotbed for fine waterfowl-related folk art. "There are so many good carvers from here," Danos says with more than a little pride. "We always had a lot of decoys around. We made them ourselves as a means of shooting birds and feeding our families. That mostly stopped when plastic decoys came out. They were easier to carry, and the old-timers couldn't sell their birds because of the plastic decoys. But the contests really brought the art of carving back."

After a few notable wins at national carving shows, suddenly the whole country knew that a group of Cajun decoy carvers were fabricating dynamic and lovely examples of one of America's oldest art forms.

When asked about the "Cajun Style," Danos just smiles. "Yeah, I like a full-bodied bird. We learned it from Jimmy Vizier. Tan also makes a big healthy looking bird. We are so lucky in this area. You don't have to go very far to get some help with a bird. We sometimes get together as a group and carve."

The carver offers several levels of finish and carving detail on his decoys because "people collect different types and grades of birds, and that way, as a carver you don't get tired of carving the same one." That also puts his work in a broad price range of $300 to $2,500 depending on the amount of work involved. It also effects delivery times, which can take from three weeks to three months.

The success and acclaim his decoys have brought him is explained simply, "I had a God-given talent that I didn't know I had. If I can do it, anybody can. At first the painting was scary. It's amazing. At first when I looked at a mallard, all I saw was a green head. Now I see blues, yellows, and violets. The smooth birds are a little more difficult to paint because the painting has to show details, and create shadows, shades, and depth on a smooth surface." Now an accomplished full-time carver who also teaches a number of classes and workshops, Danos is adding to a great tradition in Louisiana bayou-styled waterfowl sculpture.

At the Southeastern Wildlife Expo held in Charleston, South Carolina, each February, I have seen the work of many good carvers over the years. This past winter I was truly impressed by the work of Jim Robinson of Hopedale, Illinois, whose dramatic life-sized carving of a cock pheasant exploding from cover was the most impressive piece I examined. He also exhibited a carving of three teal winging in unison, connected by only their wing tips, which was outstanding. That should come as no surprise, since he has been winning accolades since his teen years. An avid outdoorsman and a practitioner of the ancient sport of falconry, he has been featured in magazines and on national network television. His carvings have won many national and world-class awards, like the A. Danner Frazer Memorial Award from the Ward World Championships for the best teenaged carver. Robinson's sculptures have been chosen three times by the Leigh Yawkey Woodson Art Museum for their prestigious "Birds in Art" exhibit, which features the best work of artists from around the world. The first time he was accepted he was only eighteen years old, the youngest ever to be invited.

Jim Sprankle, of Chester, Maryland, has been carving birds out of wood for twenty-seven years. A respected master carver, he took second place this past year in Decorative Lifesize with a carving of three green-winged teal flying over marsh grass. He can't believe he has been at it so long. "I save a bird each year," he laughed, "and there are twenty-seven of them around here. I guess they don't lie." For most of his career he has been one of the top artists in the field, with many championships over the years. He does one or two large pieces each year which sell for $25,000 to $40,000, and number of smaller single birds that go for $5,000 to $10,000. He is also involved in teaching and workshops as well as writing books on the subject and has produced a series of video tapes.

An ex-pro baseball player, he can't stand to be away too long from his carving bench. Recently when he got back from a week's vacation, he said, "I couldn't wait to get back into the shop. This is where I belong."

A growing artistic movement in carving is called Interpretive Wood Sculpture by the Ward Foundation. The carver uses a single block of walnut, cherry, or other handsome hardwood. With little or no detail burning or painting, the carver simply lets the wood itself dictate what the final form of the sculpture will be. It results in a lovely free-flowing style. John T. Sharp of Kent, Ohio, recently won Best in World at the Ward Competition, this time with an unusual but striking carving of a road-killed pheasant. Done in walnut, the piece even has the asphalt roadway carved into the design. In 1991 his walnut carving of five cormorants took the top prize. His magnificent carvings are found in several fine art galleries.

One of the most dynamic carvings to surface in recent years was a peregrine falcon diving on a swallow, carved out of walnut. It was done by David and Mary Ahrendt of Hackensack, Minnesota, and it was unique in that most of the wood was smooth and free flowing while the head and shoulders of both birds were carved, burned and painted. It caused quite a stir. The piece gives an impression of speed with detail at the same time. More of this type of artistic interpretation is sure to gain in popularity in the future.

The husband and wife team of Don and Donna Johnson of Bloomington, Minnesota, have been carving since 1985. They have won many accolades including six Best in Show awards at various shows and decoy contests. A recent carving that caught my eye was their sculpture of a bull drake canvasback diving underwater to catch a fleeing bluegill. Another of their carvings is of three buffleheads diving after snails. Both have the design and dynamics that separate just wooden birds from art.

Don works out the mechanics of each carving, and Donna does the actual woodwork and painting. Their carvings cost from

$300 for a miniature to around $2,500 to $4,500 for a major piece.

On the eastern shore of Virginia there lives a new/old master of decoy carving. Mark McNair is producing working-type decoys with the same elegant lines of the birds produced by the best carvers of yesteryear. From his shop he combines fine woodworking craftsmanship with an eye for the subtle grace to be found in such American art icons. He "ages" his birds so they have the appearance of a well-used and well-loved working decoy. The paint, wood, and even rusted nail holes have a look of valiant service in the duck marshes. They are expertly hollowed, just like many of the originals.

A transplanted Connecticut Yankee who now calls himself a Southerner, he believes the love of well-crafted implements designed for hunting and fishing transcends many different aspects of the sport.

"When I was a boy, I loved to go through my father's tackle box and look at all those wooden plugs. I thought they were great. I think the attraction to them, as well as decoys, is metaphysical. It's the same with my four-year-old son. He was looking at my tackle box and saw some old lures and was captivated. He was full of questions about them. Now all he wants to do is go fishing with them."

That is what really got McNair into decoys. He was not even a hunter when he first became enamored with them. He had gone to the Rhode Island School of Design and was looking for a means to express himself when he saw a beautiful old decoy. He knew instantly that he had to "carve one myself." He has since become an enthusiastic hunter, having been introduced to its traditions by friends.

The urgency to create in the spirit of the old master decoy carvers is reflected when you ask about his delivery times. "Oh, anywhere from the end of the week to almost never," he answers, tongue in cheek. Actually, most of his birds are done in ten days to two weeks. He is sometimes so excited about a project that he goes to his shop as soon as he gets off the phone with a customer. "I sometimes just want to do it right now," he says. But, if it is a project that he just doesn't feel strongly about, like carving a redhead decoy, which he professes to not know enough about, it may never get done. "I have one customer that is still waiting, after several years, for me to do a redhead drake for him. It has become almost a joke between us. Maybe one day."

McNair decoys are very reasonably priced considering that their workmanship and artistic interpretation is on a par with originals that cost many thousands of dollars. They sell from $250 to $850. A shorebird is $350, with diving and puddle ducks usually going for $400 to $600. A more complicated bird like a preening pintail, for example, may sell for $750 or so. This past season he even did two complete shooting rigs for happy customers. That must have given them the same satisfaction that Elmer Crowell's or Ira Hudson's customers felt when they sat in a blind and watched well-decoyed ducks flock into their spreads. It seems with McNair decoys you *can* go back to the good old days.

Not all hand-wrought wood sculptures are of waterfowl and other birds. A love of fish and fishing has led Jack Voytko, a wood carver and artist from Pittsburgh, Pennsylvania, to the forefront of the fast-growing art form of fish carving. His wood creations are strikingly realistic and artistic in their expression of the sleek power and beauty of our most beloved sport fish.

A fly fisherman by avocation, he has re-created many of the fish species he has caught. The most common are trout (rainbow, brown, and brook), steelhead, and his favorite fish, the Atlantic salmon. Others include tarpon, bonefish, permit, and even peacock bass, as well as largemouths and bluegills.

Voytko began a lifelong interest in fish and fishing as a young boy when he spent much of his high-school spending

Mark McNair's artistic decoys rival the best of the old masters.

A magnificent McNair pintail carving showing the artist's elegant and refined technique.

Jack Voytko in his studio with a carving in process.

money pursuing fish, and on their preservation by way of taxidermy. While stationed in Newfoundland as an officer in the Air
Force, he was able to enjoy many free hours angling for salmon
and trout. A later job allowed him to travel extensively from Alaska
to Central America, with a fly rod always packed in his duffel.
This knowledge and his talent as an artist has led him to illustrate
several books and magazines on fishing.

     For complete accuracy, his research includes photograph-
ing, measuring, tracing, and color sketching freshly caught fish.
He then creates exact-to-scale templates, and band saws tupelo
wood to the proper contours. Fins are carved and added sepa-
rately. The sculpture is then sealed, primed and painted with acryl-
ics, and given several coats of glossy lacquer. The result is a lovely

creation that many people think is taxidermy because of its realism. The artist prefers to work closely with his clients to maximize the accuracy of the fish they desire. Most carvings presently take around three months or so to complete and cost from $500 to $1,500. For the fisherman they are a beautiful and artful reminder of glorious days spent on the water.

WATERFOWL
CALLS

Duck call by Howard Harlan (left) and goose call by Tom Weigel (right) are handmade from beautiful exotic hardwoods.

WATERFOWL CALLS

Millions of years before prehistory the sound of their music filled the morning skies. And still each fall across North America, waterfowl begin their annual migrations, gathering into great flocks to renew an age-old pilgrimage from the northern marshes of their birth to warmer climes far to the south.

From the potholes of Manitoba to the flood plains of the Mississippi River to the rice fields and green timber of Arkansas, hunters have huddled in blinds listening to the quacks, honks, and whistles of ducks and geese and have tried to imitate their sounds and lure them into gun range.

For the last century the duck call has evolved into not only an instrument of musical quality but an art form of hand-carved native and exotic hardwoods. Fashioned into slender and sensuous shapes and polished to let the natural beauty of the wood show through, the waterfowl calls being produced today by craftsmen throughout the country are the best and most beautiful ever. Some should be considered museum pieces to be admired as a truly unique American folk art.

Duck calls began to evolve during the 1850s with the use of tonge-pincher calls. These simple instruments had no barrel and consisted of a pair of curved sound boards with a reed in the middle, essentially mimicking the construction of a real duck's sounding apparatus. Thought to have originated in England, these early calls imitated the quack of a hen mallard in the hope of luring puddle ducks into gun range.

By the 1860s a new type of call evolved in Illinois with a barrel sound chamber and cork wedge to hold the reed. Then around 1880 a fellow named Victor Glodo, who lived close to Reelfoot Lake, Tennessee, a famous waterfowl area in the middle of the Mississippi Flyway, made a call with a wooden wedge block. That in itself was significant, but he also established the duck call shape as we know it today. Perhaps more important, he was the first person to checker a call. This embellishment, similar to the handcut lines found on a fine firearm, brought duck calls firmly into the art category. Presumably this checkering, and later hand-carving and sculpting panels on the call, appealed to the "sports" who came from the population centers to sample Reelfoot Lake duck hunting. It was most certainly an artistic expression previously unseen on such a seemingly basic tool as a simple duck call. Glodo is now known as the father of the duck call; the type he originated is still made today and defined as the Reelfoot style.

Other callmakers soon followed in the Reelfoot tradition, including John "Sundown" Cochran, his son "Son" Cochran, and Sharpie Shaw. All of their calls are very collectible and valuable today. Cloyd "Sharpie" Shaw was one of the best-known Reelfoot Lake callmakers from the mid-1920s through the late-1950s and 1960s. Sharpie, like his two brothers and many of the

Collector-quality duck calls by: (from top) Kent Freeman, Sam McKoone, Rick Yagerer, James Yule, and Howard Harlan. The Harlan call is made of ivory.

folks who earned a hard living around the lake in those days, was a guide and outfitter all of his life. He worked on the calls every night when his children were growing up, even in the summertime. During the duck season he was up before daylight to guide on the lake and then stayed up until midnight to tune calls for other folks who owned his calls. A Sharpie Shaw call is now a valuable collector's item and a part of Reelfoot history.

The other great waterfowling areas saw the development of additional varieties of calls and the rise to prominence of other skilled and innovative makers. Most came from the Mississippi River Delta of the Midwest and coastal areas of the South. The Illinois-type call was further refined, and significant calls came from Louisiana and Arkansas. Why? It was simple. By the time ducks made their way through the gauntlet from the Canadian provinces of their birth to midwestern and southern gathering areas, they had heard just about every bad note a hunter could blow on a call. If you couldn't make the right notes, you just were not going to kill very many ducks.

The men who made these calls were hardy outdoorsmen, many times guides or market hunters whose livelihood depended on their ability to lure ducks. For the collector and student of waterfowl calls there are names to be found on calls that make them treasures and valuable collectibles. The early Illinois-type calls were made by craftsmen like F.A. Allen, C.W. Grubbs, George Peterson, Charles Ditto, Charles Perdew, James Reynolds, and Dick Burns. Later Illinois calls were made by Phillip S. Olt (whose hard-rubber call is the most popular in history and is made by the thousands today), August Kuhlemeier, Mark Wipple, and A.M. Bowles.

Because many of the great hordes of ducks coming down the Mississippi Flyway wintered in Arkansas, artisans like James Tillman (J.T.) Beckhart transformed the Illinois call into what is now known as the Arkansas call. Beckhart's beautiful carved and checkered calls had metal reeds, unlike the plastic reeds of present-day Arkansas calls, but his designs influenced others such that they became the blueprint of today's most popular models. Famous calling champions like Chick Major (his family still makes his line of great calls) took the basic design and carried it further.

After Glodo, Reelfoot calls evolved further from the work of callmakers like G.D. Kinny, the Cochrans, Perry Hooker, Tom Turpin, Earl Dennison, Doug and Nat Porter, and Fred Harlow. A number of craftsmen who live close to the lake today are producing Reelfoot calls on a par with those of more historic origins.

The interest in making and collecting quality waterfowl calls is at an all-time high. In 1987 the Callmakers and Collectors Association of America was formed by thirty-two enthusiasts to promote this unique American art form. That organization now numbers more than four hundred members.

A leader in this quest is callmaker and collector Howard Harlan, who lives in Nashville, Tennessee. His shop in the Home of Country Music is only a little over an hour away from Reelfoot Lake, where he maintains a permanent duck blind. A founder and past president of the

Howard Harlan blowing one of his calls at Reelfoot Lake, Tennessee.

Callmakers Association, he literally wrote the book on callmaking. By that I mean he co-authored *Duck Calls: An Enduring American Folk Art* with W. Crew Anderson. That book has become the bible for collectors and history buffs seeking knowledge on callmakers, old and new alike. The basis for such a monumental work happens to be Harlan's collection of calls from most of the best old-time and contemporary makers.

Harlan, by way of his Heavy Duty Call Company, also just happens to make fantastic calls himself. His craftsmanship has led him to first-place trophies in many callmaking competitions. He won a recent show with a magnificent carved and checkered call made entirely of ivory! It surely qualifies as a museum piece.

A callmaker for twenty-five years, he started like a lot of others. "I wanted to make the best on the market," he says with a shrug. "I started collecting everyone's call and now have over five thousand, and I'm still trying to make the best."

I met Harlan at the 1993 Reelfoot Lake Callmakers and Collectors Show and Waterfowl Festival. He took me to a dock that stuck out into the famous duck-hunting hot spot and gave a demonstration with one of his calls. As if by some divine intervention, just as he finished a series of highballs, chuckles, and quacks, in sailed a hen mallard within yards of where we were standing. He looked at me with a grin on his face. "See, I told you they would call ducks."

I procured one of his calls right then and there. It is one of the easiest calls to blow well that I've ever tried. It produces a full range of sounds with very little effort.

Heavy Duty Duck Calls are produced in metal or plastic reed versions, with a single or double reed, and are constructed out of cocobolo from South America and African blackwood, both from the rosewood family. He chooses to use these materials rather than some other popular domestic woods because they have natural oils that finish quite nicely by buffing, unlike walnut or maple, which need a coat of varnish. He feels that the oily woods assure a long life and excellent tone, exactly like the orchestral woodwind instruments that are made from the same materials.

Harlan's calls can be ordered plain or with checkered panels (custom-gun quality). Besides duck and goose calls, he also makes a nice cocobolo shotshell-style pintail-widgeon whistle. Duck calls range in price from $60 for a plain standard model to $450 for a matching set of checkered blackwood duck and goose calls with brass bands and a handmade double leather lanyard and walnut display case. No calls represent higher quality or better value.

While perusing the calls of various makers at a recent show, I noticed several extensively carved calls hanging from the neck of a fellow passing by. They were extraordinary, unlike any I had ever seen. Upon inquiry he said they had been crafted by a man by the name of James E. Yule, from Catahula, Louisiana, and that the callmaker was present at the show. I looked him up and met an artisan producing some of the most incredible pieces of folk art I have ever seen.

Yule has been making duck calls for more than forty years and still crafts a few each year as his schedule allows. A woodcarver who has specialized in portrait sculpture and western themes, he is a former rodeo cowboy, house builder, and (for many years) a teacher at several Bible colleges. He comes from a very artistic family. His grandmother was a Remington and closely related to Frederick Remington, perhaps the most famous western artist in history. Yule's Scottish grandfather was a woodworker and blacksmith, and his father was a silversmith.

The Yule calls I discovered were each a masterpiece of wood carving in addition to being fine duck calls. (They also had a distinctive elliptical mouthpiece that is another Yule trademark.) All were unique. Intricately carved Indian heads in full war bonnets, noble Mohawk warriors, ferocious looking Vikings, graceful wading birds, swimming retrieving dogs, ducks, and various other figures leapt from the polished wood. Obviously every piece took a great amount of planning and untold hours of work to complete.

Yule says it's not easy. "I let the wood talk to me. It suggests the line, color, and composition. A knot in the wood may be an eye of a dog or duck, or something else. But it is a struggle. You see it in the wood, but it resists every step of the way."

There are also certain artistic and poetic meanings to be found in the carvings. On one call there was a stoic Indian brave holding a tomahawk; on the other side a peace pipe stood out in relief. "With the two I can show the extremes of the human emotion," Yule pointed out.

For materials he uses almost any wood that speaks to him— cedar, walnut, persimmon, or even such oddities as huckleberry root. In his pocket he carried a piece of pecan wood. "I don't know what it's going to tell me. I'm still studying it," he said with a smile.

Whatever grows from the wood, it will surely be another monument to callmaking and woodcarving. Fully carved Yule calls sell for $600 and up, and they are a bargain at that price. But it may take a while to get one. You have to wait until the wood stops resisting.

Another champion carver is making phenomenal calls right in the middle of the Mississippi Flyway. Kent Freeman lives in Cape Girardeau, Missouri, close by the banks of Big Muddy. A full-time artist, he began making duck calls twenty-eight years ago and started carving decorative decoys eight years ago. His success has been remarkable.

In 1990 Freeman won first place in the World Wildfowl Carving Championship with a hen blue-wing teal carved out of tupelo. Then in 1992, the first time he entered, he took first place at the Callmakers and Collectors Association competition in the carved calls division for a matched set of duck and goose calls and best-in-show for the duck call. They illustrated intertwined snakes encircling the barrel of the call. This past year he made it two years in a row, winning first place with a gorgeous matched set of duck and goose calls carved to look exactly like the birds they are designed to call.

Most of his calls are cut from walnut using traditional hand tools and several power carving tools used by most decoy carvers. They are usually built with Arkansas-type construction, if you were ever of a mind to actually take them hunting.

Freeman learned his callmaking from someone he calls a "master callmaker," his eighth-grade teacher, Allen Bradley, Jr. His mentor also taught him a great deal about duck hunting after Freeman's father died when the artist was still a young boy. The work of the great callmaker J.T. Beckhart, who lived close to Freeman's house and made his carved and checkered collector's treasures around the turn of the century, was his artistic inspiration. All of the Missourian's art pieces start as a carefully detailed drawing to show layout and overall design. Custom orders take on average about three months to complete, and price varies according to what goes into the carving. Each, as Freeman puts it, "is an original work. They cannot be duplicated."

Jack Wilson of Flushing, Michigan, is a premier callmaker in the best tradition of the old masters. His calls range from simple hunting models to some of the finest carved and checkered masterpieces to be found today. One of the founders of the Callmakers Association, he has won many competitions with his calls, which are considered a "must buy" by many collectors.

Tom Weigel of Otley, Iowa, crafts wonderful duck and goose calls. An avid duck and goose hunter, he has been a full-time maker since 1984, although he had been doing it part-time for thirty-five years. He made callmaking a profession on the premise that you don't have to see very well to make duck calls. Tom is legally blind. He was hit by an illness in 1974 which left him with a little peripheral vision and almost none straight ahead. Yet he is one of the best callmakers in the country.

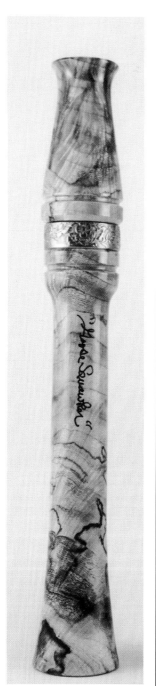

Jack Wilson flute-style goose call made of spalted hackleberry.

His shop is nestled on the shores of Lake Red Rock where he can step out his back door and practice all the sounds any duck or goose looking for companionship could ask for. He begins his calls with blocks of ebony, cocobolo, and osage orange and then, by way of sophisticated electronic measuring devices, he turns them into musical instruments.

I learned how well his calls work in a truly bizarre way. I had one of his goose calls built out of an exhibition-grade piece of cocobolo and was going to use it as a prop in a photo I was taking at a friend's rustic house in the woods. While I was unloading my equipment, my buddy, who is a professional retriever trainer and experienced waterfowler, decided to try out the call. As I stumbled into the house with my last load he was out on his patio frantically gesturing for me to come outside.

"Listen," he commanded. "Do you hear anything?" he asked, straining to hear in the gathering darkness of late autumn. I listened for a minute and then I heard it, a distant honking of Canada geese on the river at the far end of his property. "I can't believe it," he said. "I was trying out this call in the living room and thought I heard geese honking. When

I came outside, every time I honked they answered back. This is some call."

Coincidence? Maybe, but I don't think so. That call, like others of Weigel's I have heard, is one of the easiest to make sound like a goose, or flock of geese for that matter, that I have ever heard. If we had a little more time I believe we could have called them into my friend's backyard.

Weigel makes both metal- and plastic-reed duck calls and conventional and flute-style goose calls. Some of his calls are even carved into over-sized renditions of a goose head. He labels himself a callmaker, collector, and carver of folk art. Price range is $50 to $150 and he can deliver most of his styles within two to ten days. He likes his work. "People seem to like nice handmade wood calls," he reflects. "And it is easier to work at home at something I like and that is close to my favorite thing—hunting."

Ken Martin has been producing his famous Horseshoe Lake Model goose call on a full-time basis for more than thirty-five years. They are used very successfully all over North America, as are his classic duck calls. From his workshop in Olive Branch, Illinois, he completes all the steps to craft and tune the calls personally. He began carving calls as a young man in

Wilson flute-style goose call made of feather crotch white oak.

the 1930s when his family leased a hunting club near his home.

Over the years he produced calls for large mail-order companies like L.L. Bean and Cabelas, but the calls' fame grew to the point that he now builds them mostly for direct customers. The calls are constructed out of high-quality walnut and cedar. His duck call is tuned so that it can produce an excellent treble ring of the highball and the good scratchy quack of the hen mallard; the goose call is well known for its superior tone and dependability. For only three dollars to cover shipping, an owner of a Martin call can have it re-tuned at any time during its lifetime. When you purchase a call from a custom maker it's hard to beat experience. You can tell by the way he holds a call in his weathered hands that Martin has been a waterfowler for most of his life.

Over this last century great hunting and fishing areas have produced superior craftsmen that produce top-quality equipment. Stuttgart, Arkansas, is called the duck hunting capital of the world. More mallards and other ducks winter there than anywhere else on the continent. Naturally that has led to many great decoy carvers and callmakers coming from that illustrious area.

I guess it is possible to be an old hand and a newcomer at the same time when you hail from such a place. Grover Knoll

Two Tom Weigel calls.

Ken Martin's famous Horseshoe Lake duck and goose calls.

from Clarendon, Arkansas, began making his first duck calls in 1953 while a student attending Stuttgart High School, yet he just started to sell his calls in 1993. Why so long? Well, I guess it gives new meaning to the saying "meaning to get around to it."

Knoll got sidetracked by several occupations, including running a Ford dealership for seventeen years. He presently owns a car wash and is a part-time independent petroleum landman.

But duck calls kept calling him. "I made my first call on a crude wood lathe, which I still have, in a friend's blacksmith shop and made several calls. I still have one and it is very functional, but the rest were given away," he remembers.

"I suppose the desire to have a better setup to build good calls has never gone away. When I built my present home in 1976 I constructed a shop in one end of the garage for the sole purpose of building duck calls again. Then about 1980 I bought a good lathe and a duck call jig from J.R. Walton, who supplied them to many makers such as Chick Major. But it wasn't until 1993 that the shop was cleaned out and put to its intended use. I built about seventy-five calls and decided to sell them at the Reelfoot Lake Waterfowl Festival. I wanted to know if my calls could cut the mustard before making any local sales. It was a fabulous pleasure." (He did well and recently went to a show in Stuttgart where he sold every call he took.)

Knoll's calls are constructed out of bois d'arc (osage orange, a traditional duck-call wood), cedar, cocobolo, and acrylic. They sell for $35 to $100 and each usually takes about a full day to produce.

The maker has definite opinions on why handcrafting is better. "Duck callers and calling techniques are extremely complex. If everyone could make a good adaptation to a manufactured call, and the call was capable of all desired sounds, the callmaker would be left out. But, he never will be out, because if a perfect call is ever produced not everyone will be able to get what they want out of it. All calls and callers are different and the handcrafter is well suited to making the best matches. He is in a good position to not only provide quality calls, but also to assist and instruct toward the desired caller/call match."

Knoll, despite the busy life it has created, finds making duck calls worth the effort. "It is very relaxing and rewarding to work on a duck call knowing you will be proud of it whenever it is completed. No big decisions. No time demands or schedules. Just turn the wood, blow, and tune!"

Dixie Mallard call made by Don and Brenda Cahill in the tradition of Chick Major.

In the same town of Clarendon, Arkansas, Alvin Taylor has been making superior duck calls for fifteen years. They have been used by many hunters and contest winners. A self-taught maker, it didn't hurt to grow up in a region that is famous for its duck hunting. He builds out of several different hardwoods as well as acrylic, and his calls are priced in the range of $35 to $125. When asked why a handcrafted call is better, he puts it

Fred Weeks carved and checkered Reelfoot Lake style call.

simply. "Machines and molds cannot hear. Building by hand and having a good ear is the only way to produce quality."

When you put a professional woodworker and a love for duck hunting together you have the basic ingredients for a great callmaker. Fred Weeks of Savannah, Tennessee, a cabinetmaker and patternmaker, started duck hunting in 1970, and he thought it would be nice to make calls that suited himself and his friends. His avocation has progressed into a business. I saw an array of his calls at Reelfoot, and they exhibited the quality workmanship and the clean lines of the past masters. Made of extremely high quality walnut, ebony, and cocobolo, his paneled and checkered calls were on a par with the best to be found. Prices are from $75 to $250 for a full-blown carved/checkered model.

The first honest-to-goodness quality duck call I ever owned was called the Dixie Mallard made in Arkansas by Don and Brenda Cahill, of Sherril, Arkansas. Brenda is the daughter of the famous callmaker Chick Major, who was a legend throughout the South.

That call, which I still have, is one of the easiest to blow well of any I have ever seen. Built from Osage, it has mellowed into a beautiful amber color and it will call mallards just as well today as it did when I got it many years ago. If you would like to own one of the best bargains in all of outdoor sports, they still sell them for $30 to $40.

In Albertville, Alabama, Don Perrault started to make duck calls because he wanted something that would "really bring them in." His single-reed Arkansas-type callers are built with or without brass bands out of cocobolo, osage, and other exotic woods. One unique call he makes shows the white sapwood contrasting with the deep red-purple of cocobolo. It makes for a very distinctive call. He also produces excellent widgeon-pintail whistles.

Influenced by makers such as Howard Harlan, he not only wanted to make calls to attract ducks, but also started his Grey Sky Calls business so he would be able to trade calls with other makers. He says it isn't just about making money. "It is not simply about a company making a product for profit. It has heart. It's the sweat and love of an individual poured into a sport they love."

SOURCES

RODMAKERS

Marc Aroner
P.O. Box 81
Conway, MA 01341
413-773-9920

Thomas & Thomas
2 Avenue A
Turners Falls, MA 01376
413-863-9727

Joe Saracione
P.O. Box 372
Sandy, OR 97055
503-668-3014

R.W. Summers
90 River Road East
Traverse City, MI 49684
616-946-7923

Art Weiler
313 East St.
Bound Brook, NJ 08805
908-469-9496

Douglas Kulick
Kane Klassics
P.O. Box 8124
Freemont, CA 94537
510-487-8545

Mike Clark
P.O. Box 981
Lyons, CO 80540-0981
303-823-6402

Orvis
Historic Route 7A
P.O. Box 798
Manchester, VT
05259-0798
800-548-9548

R. L. Winston Rod Co.
Drawer T
Twin Bridges, MT 59754
406-684-5674

Hardy USA
10 Godwin Place
Midland Park, NJ 07432
201-481-7557

The Powell Rod Co., Inc.
P.O. Box 4000
1152 W 8th Ave
Chico, CA 95927-4000
916-345-3393

D. G. Schroeder Rod Co.
3822 Brunswick Lane
Janesville, WI 53546
608-752-1520

Darryll Whitehead
611 Northwest 48th St.
Seattle, WA 98107
206-781-0133

W. E. Carpenter
Box 52
Huntington Mills, PA
18622
717-477-3252

Ron Kusse
Rena Marie Circle
Washington, NY 10992
914-496-7187

R. D. Taylor
P.O. Box 54
169 Avenue A
Turners Falls, MA 01376
413-863-8608

Jenkins Rod Co.
5735 South Jericho Way
Aurora, CO 80015
303-699-9128

Stephen-Stuart
Box 544, Sherman Rd.
Chester, CA 96020
916-259-2849

Wayne Cattanach
15315 Apple Ave,
Casnovia, MI 49318
616-657-5894

REELMAKERS

Stanley Bogdan
33 Fifield Street
Nashua, NH 03060

Robbie Jansen
Seamaster Corporation
16115 S.W. 117th Ave.
Unit A-8
Miami, FL 33177-1614
305-253-2408

Joe Saracione
P.O. Box 372
Sandy, OR 97055
503-668-3014

Billy Pate Reels
Ted Juracsik Tool & Die
900 N.E. 40th Ct.
Oakland Park, FL 33334
305-566-0222

Abel
165 Aviador St.
Camarillo, CA 93010
805-482-0701

Tycoon Fin- Nor
2921 S.W. 31st Ave.
Hallandale, FL
33009-2031
305-966-5507

Bill Ballan
Carmans River Reel
Company
230 Seaman Ave.
Bayport, NY 11705
516-472-0744

Bob Corsetti
Peerless
427-3 Amherst St.
Suite 177
Nashua, NH 03063
603-595-2458

REELMAKERS

Bill Adams
91 Fairfax St
West Haven, CT 06516
203-937-6509

Ted Godfrey
3509 Pleasant Plains Dr.
Reistertown, MD 21136
410-239-8468

FLIES

Charlton
1179-A Water Tank Rd.
Burlington, WA 98233
206-757-2609

Jim Stewart
Stewart's Designer Flies
1104 S. Dunbar Ave.
Tampa, Fl 33629

Greg Snyder
King Neptune's Flies
P.O. Box 67101
Phoenix, AZ 85082
602-949-1927

Billy Munn
Rt. 1, Box 148
Bridgeport, TX 76026
817-683-4512

Del Mazza
2609 Genesee Street
Utica, NY 13501
315-733-4593

Paul Schmookler
The Complete Sportsman
P.O. Box 540104
Millis, MA 02054
508-376-6276

Bob Veverka
P.O. Box 353,
Underhill, VT 05489
802-899-2049

NETS & BOXES

Craig Brown Woodwork
11744 US Highway 31 S.
Elk Rapids, MI
49629-0487
616-264-6000

Ron Reinhold
4446 Westridge Dr.
Williamsburg, MI 49690
616-938-9211

KNIFEMAKERS

Knifemakers Guild
P.O. Box 83A
Route 6, Box 83A
Santa Fe, NM 87501

American Bladesmith
Society
Joseph G. Cordova-
Treasurer
P.O. Box 977
Peralta, NM 87042

George Herron
Route, Box 25A
Springfield, SC 29146
803-258-3914

Corbet Sigman
Route 1, Box 212-A
Liberty, WV 25124
304-586-9131

Don Fogg
Rt. 6, Box 107
Jasper, AL 35501
205-483-0822

Daniel Winkler
P.O. Box 2166
Blowing Rock, NC 28605
704-295-9156

Tommy Lee
1011 Grassy Pond Rd.
Gaffney, SC 29340
803-489-6699

Joseph Keeslar
RR 1, Box 252
Almo, KY 42020
502-753-7919

Alex Daniels
1416 County Rd. 415
Twon Creek, AL 35672
205-685-0943

Jay Hendrickson
4294 Ballenger Creek
Pike
Frederick, MD 21701

Randall Knives
Gary Randall
P.O. Box 1988
Orlando, FL 32802

Bill Moran
P.O. Box 68
Braddock Heights, MD
21714

Bob Loveless
P.O. Box 7836
Riverside, CA 92503
714-689-7800

Lile Handmade Knives
2721 S. Arkansas Ave.
Russellville, AR 72801
501-968-2011

Ralph Dewey Harris
2607 Bell Shoals Rd.
Brandon, FL 33511
813-681-5293

Frank Centofante
P.O. Box 928
Madisonville, TN
37354-0928
615-442-5767

Ray Cover
Rt. 1, Box 194
Mineral Point, MO
63660
314-749-3783

RIFLEMAKERS

American Custom
Gunmakers Guild
P.O. Box 812
Burlington, IA 52601-0812

D'Arcy Echols
164 West 580 South
Providence, UT 84332
801-753-2367

Kenny Jarrett
383 Brown Rd.
Jackson, SC 29831
803-471-3616

Paul and Sharon Dressel
209 North 92nd Ave.
Yakima, WA 98908
509-966-9233

Jere Eggleston
400 Saluda Ave.
Columbia, SC 29205
803-799-3402

MUZZLELOADERS

Mike Gervais
3804 South Cruise Dr.
Salt Lake City, UT 84109
801-277-7729

Ron Ehlert
1066 New Sheboss Rd.
Duck River, TN 38454
615-285-2622

Jim Chambers
Rt. 1, Box 513A
Candler, NC 28715
704- 667-8361

Mike Gahagan
Rt. 1, Box 352
Leicester, NC 28748
704-683-2910

Mike Ehinger
Rt. 2, Box 293 D
Steadman, NC 28391
919-531-3401

Bob Harn
228 Pensacola Rd.
Venice, FL 34285
813-488-3418

John Bergman
Rt. 2, Box 128
Puryear, TN 38251
901-247-5899

Jack Garner
P.O. Box 1175
Cornith, MS 38834
601-286-5014

Gerald Dukes
1027 Albany Ave.
Waycross, GA 31501
912-283-3090

Ted Hatfield
Hatfield Gun
224 N. Fourth Street
St. Joseph, MO 64501

LONGBOWS & RECURVES

Black Widow Custom Bows
1201 Eaglecrest
Nixa, MO 65714
417-725-3113

Howard Hill Archery
248 Canyon Creek Road
Hamilton, MT 59840
406-363-1359

Jeffery Archery
821 Pepper St.
P.O. Box 9625
Columbia, SC 29290
803-776-3832

J. D. Berry Archery
Designs
South 6511 Plymouth Rd.
Spokane, WA 99204
509-624-3317

Jim Brackenbury, Inc.
8326 S.E. 252nd Ave.
Gresham, OR 97080
503-666-1667

Shawnee Traditions
Rt. 2, Box 414
Marion, Illinois 62959

John Schultz
Appalachian Archery
Dave Guthrie, Bower
17 Stonegate Estates
Sandyville, WV 25275
304-372-4918

Custom Stickbows by Fox
701 East Hwy 82
Wallowa, OR 97885
503-886-9110

Great Northern
Longbow Co.
201 N. Main
Nashville, MI 49073
517-852-0820

Welchman Longbow
Company
Prince of Wales Island -
Whale Pass
P.O. Box W.W.P.
Ketchikan, Alaska 99950-
0280

Dan Quillan's Archery
Traditions
196 Alps Rd.
Athens, GA 30606
706-543-1893

Robertson Stykbow
Hwy 87 West
Box 329
Lewistown, MT 59547
406-538-2818

The Spirit Longbow
Company
5513 Third Street
Tillamook, OR 97141
503-842-4944

Elburg Archery
Route 7, Box 301
Madison, IN 47250
812-866-5285

Cascade Mt. Archery
Fred Anderson
E 750 Krabbenhoft
Grapeview, WA 98546
206-426-8634

Bighorn Archery
King of the Mountain
Sports
2709 W. Eisenhower Blvd.
Loveland, CO 80537
303-962-9306

LONGBOWS & RECURVES

Jack Smith
Blackhawk Bows
Route 1, Box 348
Princeton, IL 61356
815-875-1695

Chuck Jones
Okaw Valley Long Bows
Rt. 2, Box 57
Vandalia, IL 62471
618-283-2866

CARVERS

Ward Museum of
Wildfowl Art
909 S. Schumaker Dr.
Salisbury, MD 21801
401-742-4988

Grainger McKoy
490 Hwy. 261 N.
Sumpter, SC 29154

J.D. Voytko
214 Sunridge Dr.
Pittsburgh, PA 15238
412-828-3497

Jim Robinson
RR #1, Box 106/c
Hopedale, IL 61747
309-449-3296

John T. Sharp
6949 Rt. 43
Kent, OH 44240
216-678-0227

Don and Donna Johnson
10557 Decatur Ave. South
Bloomington, MN 55438
612-944-1613

Jim Sprankle
1147 Golden Olive Ct.
Sanibel Island, FL 33957
813-472-8666

Carl Danos
Rt. 1, Box 113 Virginia St.
Lockport, LA 70374
504-693-7462
Larry Barth
256 Haugerhood Rd.
Stahlstown, PA 16567
412-593-7128

Pat Godin
P.O. Box 62
Brantford, Ontario, Canada
N3T 5M3

Tan and Jude Brunet
P.O. Box 312
Galliano, LA 70354
504-632-2465

Jett Brunet
P.O. Box 2243
West 150th St.
Galliano, LA 70354
504-632-2324

David and Mary Ahrendt
Box 132C
Hackensack, MN 56452
218-682-2080

Mark McNair
Island Neck
Craddockville, VA 23341
804-442-5628

WATERFOWL CALLMAKERS

Howard Harlan/
Callmakers & Collectors
Association of America
Heavy Duty Call Co.
4920 Franklin Rd.
Nashville, TN 37220
615-832-0564

Tom Weigel
RR1, Box 71A

Otley, IA 50214
515-842-6907
James E. Yule
H.C. 60, Box 143
Jena, LA 71342
318-992-4040

Kent Freeman
843 N. Cape Rock Dr.
Cape Girardeau, MO
63701
314-335-2256

Ken Martin
Box 279
Olive Branch, IL 62969
618-776-5603

Fred Weeks
200 South Fairground St.
Savannah, TN 38372
901-925-1030

Alvin Taylor
328 South 2nd St.
Clarendon, AR 72029
501-747-5479

Don and Brenda Cahill
9018 Trulok Bay
Sherril, AR 72152
501-535-5419

Don Perrault
520 Rose Rd. Apt. 304
Albertville, AL 35950
205-878-9871

Grover Knoll
P.O. Box 275
Clarendon, AR
72029-0275
501-747-5491

Jack Wilson
5145 Deland Rd.
Flushing, MI 48433
313-659-3676